The Write Type

Discover Your True
Writer's Identity
and Create a
Customized Writing Plan

Karen E. Peterson, Ph.D.
AUTHOR OF *Write.*

adamsmedia
avon, massachusetts

Published by
Adams Media, an F+W Publications Company
57 Littlefield Street, Avon, MA 02322. U.S.A.
www.adamsmedia.com

ISBN 10: 1-59869-470-7
ISBN 13: 978-1-59869-470-3

Printed in the United States of America.

J I H G F E D C B A

Library of Congress Cataloging-in-Publication Data
is available from the publisher.

This publication is designed to provide accurate and authoritative information with regard
to the subject matter covered. It is sold with the understanding that the publisher is not
engaged in rendering legal, accounting, or other professional advice. If legal advice or
other expert assistance is required, the services of a competent professional person should
be sought.

> —From a *Declaration of Principles* jointly adopted by a Committee of the
> American Bar Association and a Committee of Publishers and Associations

Many of the designations used by manufacturers and sellers to distinguish their product
are claimed as trademarks. Where those designations appear in this book and Adams
Media was aware of a trademark claim, the designations have been printed with initial
capital letters.

The author has written this book to provide accurate and authoritative information with
regard to the subject matter covered. It is sold with the understanding that the author is
not engaged in rendering mental health services or any other professional services. Neither
this book, nor the exercises included in this book, is intended as a substitute for psychotherapy. If mental health treatment is required, the services of a competent mental health
professional should be sought.

This book is available at quantity discounts for bulk purchases.
For information, please call 1-800-289-0963.

And I urge you to please notice when you are happy, and exclaim or murmur or think at some point, 'If this isn't nice, I don't know what is.'

KURT VONNEGUT, *Man Without a Country*

Contents

###

Acknowledgments

I would like to take this opportunity to thank all of those who have helped in the creation of this book. I am indebted to the theorists and researchers who have pioneered the areas of brain functioning, writing as therapy, and Gestalt language awareness.

I am grateful, as always, to my agent, Linda L. Roghaar, for her support, sense of humor, patience, understanding, and wisdom.

I would also like to thank my editor at Adams Media, Paula Munier, as well as the rest of the staff at Adams Media, for their patience, encouragement, and support of my writing.

Thanks also to Christine Belleris, who first believed in my work. A special thank-you goes out to Lisa Ellis—my friend/kindred spirit/perpetual encourager—who often believed more in my ideas than I could at the time. Thank you also to Daniela Roher and Kimberly Gregson, for your encouragement from one writer to another. I also thank my friend Abby Nelson for her wit, wisdom, and whimsy—and the hand-painted rabbit. Just because.

I am deeply grateful to the members of my family for their kindness and encouragement and thoughtful guidance when I needed them most: Norma Carreras—the real lady in red, who knows the true meaning of family, Nicolas Carreras—who knows the true meaning of whimsy, and Steve Carreras, who helped me get it right this time.

And a very special and eternal *thank-you* goes out to the very gracious Mr. Kurt Vonnegut, who said in his last book, "All I really wanted to do was give people the relief of laughing. . . . If a hundred years from now, people are still laughing, I'd certainly be pleased." Well, I'm here to tell you, old chum, they're still laughing. And they always will be.

CHAPTER 1

What Kind of Writer Are You?

If you were a member of Jesse James's band and people asked you what you were, you wouldn't say 'Well, I'm a desperado.' You'd say something like 'I work in banks' or 'I've done some railroad work.' It took me a long time just to say 'I'm a writer.' It's really embarrassing.

ROY BLOUNT, JR.

I think I did pretty well, considering I started out with nothing but a bunch of blank paper.

STEVE MARTIN

The Supposed-to Syndrome

As I autograph her book, here's what the woman in the lovely lime-green tank top says to me: "I started writing every day, like you're supposed to, but I couldn't stick with it so I stopped writing. I guess I'm just not a writer."

Though I can't say it, I'm thinking, *Definitely an "S"—I hope my book helps her.*

And here's what the young man in the tangy lemon-yellow T-shirt says: "I started writing first thing in the morning, like you're supposed to, but I couldn't keep it up so I stopped. I'm not really a writer."

Definitely a "P."

As for the man in the white shirt and dapper blue-striped tie: "I'd like to write my novel, you know, get away from it all for a month or two like you're supposed to and crank out a first draft. But I can never get away from the office long enough, so I just don't get time to write."

Sounds like an "LC" to me.

And here's what the ponytailed college student in the gray baggy sweats says: "I tried to get myself to write by meditating first in a quiet place like you're supposed to, but I couldn't stand the silence because I have to be practically manic to write, and since I'm never in the right mood, I just don't write."

A quintessential "H," no doubt, as writers go.

It may seem odd that in an instant I am categorizing these writers into types—a "Sporadic" writer, a "PM" writer, a "Log Cabin" writer, and a "Hyped" writer—but that's what I do. In helping writers find their way to the page, I first focus on their natural instincts. Then, I help them to determine if they actually *like* their usual patterns—in other words, have they chosen these patterns, or were these patterns instilled by default at the hands of parents, former teachers, advisors, or good old DNA? Finally, I help writers to synchronize (and/or change) their pre-existing writing rhythms to fit into their current lifestyles. However, as you probably noticed in reading about the four writers above, the one element they all have in common is what I call the "Supposed-to Syndrome." They don't feel they can call themselves "writers" unless they write the way they're *supposed to*, however that may be defined, so they don't write at all. Although they don't know it yet, they *are* writers, by definition, simply because they *want to write.*

As writers, we're exposed to so many books that tell us how we should approach the writing process. One says to write in the morning, but what if you're a night owl? Another may prescribe a relaxed daily time for writing, but what if you're a sporadic, deadline-driven writer? Although these approaches may work for some writers, most writers don't seem to fit into any one category. What works for one writer becomes paralyzing for the next.

For example, many well-known authors have shared their strategies for success: writing from 5 to 10 A.M.; writing in the afternoon; writing from 9 to 5 with an hour for lunch; writing only on weekends; writing while listening to music; writing in your pajamas; or, as Victor Hugo used to do, writing only after surrendering his clothing to his valet, who was not to return until the day's writing had been completed. You name it, and just about every suggestion possible is out there. Perhaps with the exception of Victor Hugo's strategy, these are all viable options, but how do you know which one is right for *you*?

Is Your Type *Set*?

With all this talk about "type," we may feel stymied no matter which way we turn. In other words, most people feel that their writing type is set—predetermined and unchangeable. However, this type of thinking (pun intended) would be analogous to a twenty-first century writer insisting on using a manual typewriter instead of a word processing program on a computer.

Sure, typewriters deliver the old-fashioned charm of the staccato snap of metal key against paper, the tiny bell ringing when you've hit your margin, the zipping sound at the return of the carriage. On the other hand, we're talking about a pretty rigid system of communication.

When I think about whether my own writing "type" is set, the first thing I think of is the word "typeset," as in Gutenberg's first printing press, which then reminds me of those archaic machines known as manual typewriters, which is what I grew up on. Talk about having difficulty making a change!

In the early days of manual typewriters, you'd have to type the entire page over again if you made a mistake. Then came erasable paper, a translucent alternative that, upon reinsertion—assuming you hadn't torn a hole in the page with your frantic erasure—had to be lined up so that the typewriter key would strike exactly where you'd made your mistake (of course, even if you could line up that "m" where you once had typed an "n," you'd still have to toss out that piece of carbon paper you'd hoped would serve as your second copy). Then came the revolutionary inventions of white correcting tape (which inevitably led to a tangled web for me), white correction fluid (easier, yes, but messier, especially if you typed over that white glob that had appeared to be dried), and finally self-correcting electric typewriters (which were much better, except for those of us who didn't notice errors until *after* removing the page from the machine, which meant it was back to square one with the same alignment problem of reinserting papers into manual typewriters).

So, when it comes to changing or reshaping your writing type, which one is it—that aggravating white correction tape, or the ease of a binary-driven machine? Well, for most of us, the answer can go either way. You may find it difficult to change the time of day that you write, but perhaps, after reading this book, you might find it easier to write in smaller chunks of time, regardless of your mood. The point is that your writing type has many components to it, and sometimes just changing one or two of them can jump-start your writing.

Here's the Fix

You need to discover your own natural writing instincts, and then learn how to manage these patterns within your current lifestyle.

There are ten components to a writer's type:

1. Level of commitment
2. Level of energy
3. Level and type of organization
4. Internal versus external motivation
5. Amount of time
6. Time of day
7. Tolerance for solitude
8. Amount and type of structure
9. Need for variety
10. Tolerance for public scrutiny

In this book, I'm inviting you to explore, shape, and implement each of these ten components of your writing type into the parameters of your current lifestyle.

Here's the good news: You actually do know what's right for you. On some level, consciously or unconsciously, you know which strategies are most appealing to you, but you haven't been able to clarify your natural patterns of writing, or perhaps your natural writing instincts just don't fit into your current lifestyle.

That's where this book can help. For example, although many writers intuitively know whether they are naturally "A.M." writers or "P.M." writers, they may not follow their natural, instinctive writing rhythm for one or more reasons:

1. It goes against what certain writing guides prescribe.
2. It conflicts with their current lifestyle.
3. It conflicts with the ghosts of edicts past (or present) delivered by parents, former teachers, editors—anyone whose vote still counts in writers' minds, consciously or unconsciously.

Accordingly, this book provides what I call the "bi-vocal approach," tapping into the voices of both the left (conscious) and the right (unconscious) side of the brain to help readers discover—and finally choose—their own particular rhythms for writing.

What most writers don't realize is that it doesn't matter where you may fall on the continuum of writing patterns (for example, maybe you're a 9 on a 10-point scale that measures how much energy you need to write). What matters is how flexible you can be in using both the right and the left side of your brain to bargain with your natural rhythms for writing—given the limits of your work, family, and other responsibilities.

For example, I used to feel that I needed to be practically manic (a 10) in order to write. All efforts were made to get myself so focused so that my writing would just flow effortlessly. However, you know the drill: I could never seem to achieve that ideal state of focus, so I just didn't write. On the other hand, now that I've learned how to practice what I preach, I'll usually settle for a 5 on that energy scale (as chosen by my logical left brain), even though the demanding, all-or-nothing right side of my brain still thinks I need at least a 9 in order to stay alert enough to put pen to paper.

In the following chapters, you'll learn how to discern which side of your brain has been running the show when it comes to writing, and which side of your brain can help you to stop the self-sabotage that thwarts so many of us when we try to access the radar screen of creativity. You probably have at least some, if not many, blips of literary brilliance on that screen, and this book is designed to help you claim them once and for all.

If you don't, who will?

And the best part about all this? You get to write without having to sacrifice the rest of your life. Remember, your writing "type" may be more fluid than you think. Each of the components of your writing type can be coalesced into a sort of rhythm—a balanced beat that's *synchronized* with all the other elements in your life: family, friends, school, work—you name it. All of these are important, and the key here is to establish a sense of balance. I'm not talking about balancing on a tightrope eighty feet in the air—just a simple plan to allow you to ease into your role as a writer.

Right now, you're probably thinking, *"I think I can do this, but it's going to be difficult, because of _____, _____, and _____."* Well, it may be easier than you think. Let's take one component of your writing patterns at a time, and see which ones you may want to shapeshift into something you can live with.

#

CHAPTER 2

Committed or Conflicted?

You must not suppose, because I am a
man of letters, that I never tried to earn an
honest living.

GEORGE BERNARD SHAW
- -

Plato: To do is to be.
Socrates: To be is to do.
Sinatra: Do be do be do.

KURT VONNEGUT
- - - - - - - - - - - - - - - - - -

How about that Day Job?

Someone commented just the other day that it must have been easy for me to write this book, since I've already written two others. Not true.

I was at once reminded of the wise words bestowed upon me by one of my clinical supervisors back in graduate school. As I lamented the fact that I—a psychology doctoral intern!—was struggling terribly with the aftermath of a relationship break-up, Dr. Clarke Carney said to me, "Do you honestly think that the plumber's pipes don't freeze in the winter?" I thought about this for a moment, and then laughed out loud at my egotistical assumption that I wasn't supposed to have any problems.

I'm not exempt from the human condition, or from any of the dilemmas discussed in this book. That's why I share some of my own responses to the exercises in this book. I'm a psychologist who happens to be a writer, and I am a writer who happens to be a psychologist. However, at this point in my life, I can think of myself as both psychologist and writer, and that feels just fine. But I didn't always feel this way. I struggled with my sense of identity: Did I come here to help others, or did I hit the planet running so I could express myself through writing? Or both?

Many people cannot fathom the thought of having two vocations. They think that Vocation #1 + Vocation #2 = Chaos. This is especially true for writers. On the one hand, we want to be able to call ourselves "writers," but, since someone has to pay the bills, we may call ourselves "office managers," "waitresses/waiters," "real estate agents," or "nurses"—whatever title is attached to what we *do* most of the day. But what we *do* does not define us. What we do is not the same as who we are: writers at heart.

Right about now, you're probably thinking, *"Yeah, right, how dare I call myself a writer when I haven't even written anything yet?"* Or, if you are writing full-time, you may be thinking, *"I can't call myself a writer—I haven't published anything yet."*

I remember thinking this way. On the other hand, so what if the rest of the world won't call you a "writer" unless you've published your work? And so what if you haven't even written a word? I am here to tell you that **if you *want to write*, then you are, by definition, a writer**—even if you spend your waking hours shuffling other people's paperwork while you yearn for a month away in a secluded cabin to write the Great American Novel.

Take a look at the following list. See if you can match these well-known writers with their original day jobs.

1.	William Carlos Williams	**a.**	professional drummer
2.	Bret Harte	**b.**	senior editor for publisher
3.	Margaret Atwood	**c.**	physician
4.	John Barth	**d.**	waiter/waitress and camp counselor
5.	Toni Morrison	**e.**	insurance company executive
6.	Wallace Stevens	**f.**	secretary of the U.S. Mint and American consul at Glasgow

Well, here are the answers:

1. c **2.** f **3.** d **4.** a **5.** b **6.** e

Surprised?

Yes, William Carlos Williams wrote his stellar poetry while maintaining his lifelong job as a pediatrician. Bret Harte wrote some of his most famous poetry while serving as secretary of the U.S. Mint in San Francisco. Margaret Atwood, one of the finest writers of our time, started out as a waitress and as a summer camp counselor. Novelist John Barth was indeed a professional drummer before he landed on his feet in the literary world. Prior to writing fiction—let alone winning a Pulitzer Prize and the Nobel Prize for literature—Toni Morrison worked as a senior editor at Random House. And, last but not least, Wallace Stevens worked as an executive for a major insurance company in Hartford, Connecticut.

Now, let's take a look at this next list.

1.	Janice Wharton	**a.**	hematologist
2.	Robert Hallman	**b.**	engineer
3.	Anthony Caravelli	**c.**	teacher
4.	Alicia Perez	**d.**	cashier
5.	Margaret Kolinsky	**e.**	stay-at-home mom
6.	Morgan Jaspers	**f.**	accountant

And the answers? Well, that's up to you. To my knowledge, none of these names belong to a successful writer. I just made them up. And that is precisely my point: couldn't your name just as easily be on such a list?

I call this "The Do-Be or Not Do-Be" list (with apologies to Mr. Vonnegut). Although you may dream of being on the bestseller list, you need to be on this "Do-Be" list first. In other words, whatever you are *doing* (day job) doesn't have to thwart your *be-ing* (writer). Of the numerous writers I have worked with over the years, many of them knew they wanted to be writers from an early age—they sensed, on some level, that writing was a part of their "being."

To Write, or Not to Write

I've worked with so many writers who have struggled with inner conflict about their writing identities. For example, one man— I'll call him Bob*—could not bring himself to finish, let alone publish, a story for which he had received kudos from a well-known author during a writer's workshop. As I explored Bob's reasons for holding himself back, it became clear that, in his family of origin, no one was allowed to outshine Bob's father. Bob's father had spent a considerable amount of time trying to become a published author, but to no avail. This, of course, left Bob stewing in a quagmire of guilt and procrastination. He even feared using a pseudonym, convinced as he was that his father might somehow recognize Bob's fiction if it were ever published.

However, as we delved deeper into Bob's reasoning, he began to understand that his belief in his father's alleged omniscience was nothing but a cognitive remnant from Bob's contentious childhood. In reality, he was now a grown man, and there was

---

*Please note that, in order to protect clients' confidentiality, all case examples in this book are composites, and all names are fictitious.

no way his father could discover Bob's pseudonymous writings. Needless to say, once Bob was able to let go of this childhood "magical thinking," he had great fun coming up with a pseudonym that suited him just fine, thank you very much.

Other writers with whom I have worked have struggled with more of an external form of conflict. For example, one man was so perplexed about how to please all of his bickering dissertation committee members that he just stopped writing. Of course, as is often the case, the committee members had different views, different agendas, and different ways of communicating all this to Jake. It didn't help that Jake had grown up in a household where conflict just wasn't addressed. As he learned to accept the fact that conflict is normal, Jake also began to learn how to deal with conflict without so much anxiety. He was able to negotiate what he needed from his dissertation advisor to create a reasonably agreeable coalition on the committee. Once that was done, Jake started writing again. You can call him "Dr. Jake" now.

As part of my work with Bob and Jake, I gave them techniques to scrutinize factors that might be contributing to their lack of commitment to the writing process. Here is one of these techniques. Let's see how you feel about being a writer. Try to fill in the blank lines with your first, gut-instinct answers.

When I think of being a writer, I think:

When I think of being a writer, I feel:

Notice any similarities or differences between your responses to this exercise. Do your answers surprise you, or do they express what you already know about your identity as a writer?

Whenever I respond to this sort of exercise, I find out something new—or confirm something familiar—with my responses. For example, for this exercise, my responses today were as follows:

When I think of being a writer, I think:

it's fun and challenging

When I think of being a writer, I feel:

lost, sometimes

Notice that I said "my responses for today"—in other words, my responses may change over the course of a few days, weeks, or months. Either way, these responses are both very different than what I would have written many years ago. In the past, I would have written "I think I'm an imposter," and "I feel stuck"— thereby reflecting my discomfort with really calling myself a writer, especially since I'd had writer's block for ten long years!

On the other hand, my responses today indicate that I enjoy being a writer although, like most human beings, I can still feel "lost" or uncertain at times—but not enough to stop me from writing.

Now, let's try the second part of this exercise. Let's see what happens when you switch hands. Try to answer these questions with your other (nondominant) hand. The idea here is not to simply repeat what you wrote above, but to just allow the pen to rest in your other hand for a moment, and see what pops up. (You may have to scrawl like a 5-year-old, but this isn't about penmanship.)

When I think of being a writer, I think:

When I think of being a writer, I feel:

Again, examine your answers for similarities or discrepancies. Do the responses surprise you? Do you notice any trends in terms of how you "think" versus how you "feel" about being a writer?

Compare your answers to the ones you wrote moments ago with your dominant hand. Does one hand disagree with the other? Does one hand present with a more childlike voice, or sound angry, sad, scared, lonely, silly, playful, or rebellious? Does one hand present with a more judgmental or rigid tone? These are just a few of the many qualities you may notice in your responses to this exercise. For example, here are my responses today provided by my nondominant hand:

When I think of being a writer, I think:

it's a good thing to do

When I think of being a writer, I feel:

happy and scared

It's pretty obvious what the trends are here for me. I tend to *think* that writing is an enjoyable and noble endeavor. However, I tend to *feel* uncertain or even scared when it comes to being a writer—and yet happy nonetheless. Where do these different voices come from? How can I feel so differently in response to the same questions? Well, let me just say that I'm not surprised at the inconsistencies in my responses. Of course I think writing is good—why else would I write? Similarly, it's not surprising that my emotional response to this exercise reflects that I may at times feel lost or even scared—words that could describe the way I often felt as a child. Alternatively, I also can say that I feel happy when I do finally sit down to write.

No matter what our responses are, as soon as we switch to our nondominant hands, we are suddenly—at least theoretically—dealing with the nondominant side of the brain. I call this technique *parallel monologue*, which is part of the bi-vocal approach I have developed to help us to understand ourselves, especially in terms of conflicting thoughts or feelings. (For a more thorough discussion of this concept and its theoretical and clinical origins, please see my previous book, *Write: 10 Days to Overcome Writer's Block. Period.*) When we answer the same question twice—once with the dominant hand, and then with the nondominant hand—we are usually accessing the two different hemispheres of the brain.

Right Brain, Left Brain

In general, the right side of the brain controls the left side of the body, and vice versa. The majority of people (85 percent) are right-handed, and are therefore left-brain dominant. However, even left-handed individuals (who are split fifty-fifty between being truly right-brain dominant versus being of mixed brain dominance) must contend with two sides of the brain—which tend to disagree about when, where, and how we should write.

In general, the "just-do-it" left side of the brain is logical, language-based, and adultlike. It can therefore conceptualize a task (e.g., writing an essay) as being composed of subtasks (e.g., reading, outlining, writing, editing). On the other hand, the generally more childlike "I-want-it-all-now" right side of the brain is dominant for emotions and the five senses. It tends to view tasks holistically, rather than in parts, and therefore can become overwhelmed at the thought of doing something as complicated as writing.

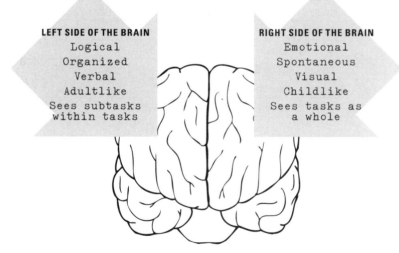

LEFT SIDE OF THE BRAIN
Logical
Organized
Verbal
Adultlike
Sees subtasks
within tasks

RIGHT SIDE OF THE BRAIN
Emotional
Spontaneous
Visual
Childlike
Sees tasks as
a whole

Regardless of which side of your brain is dominant, what is most important here is noticing any clues that might help you change your usual expectations about the writing process.

Let's take a step further in this battle between the two sides of the brain. Check off any answers that seem accurate to you, first with your dominant hand and then with your nondominant hand.

	DOMINANT HAND
1.	I'll never be able to write like a successful author.
2.	I can't keep up the habit long enough to produce anything good.
3.	My life is too busy to make time to write.
4.	If I made the commitment, my lifestyle would have to change.
5.	I can't sit still long enough to write.
6.	I worry about others criticizing me, the way _ _ _ _ _ _ _ _ _ _ _ _ did.
	NONDOMINANT HAND
1.	I'll never be able to write like a successful author.
2.	I can't keep up the habit long enough to produce anything good.
3.	My life is too busy to make time to write.
4.	If I made the commitment, my lifestyle would have to change.
5.	I can't sit still long enough to write.
6.	I worry about others criticizing me, the way _ _ _ _ _ _ _ _ _ _ _ _ did.

Let's take a moment to examine your responses. Note any differences among the items checked off by your dominant hand as opposed to the items checked off by your nondominant hand. It's common for people to respond differently—keeping in mind that the left brain tends to respond more like a logical adult while the right brain is more emotional and childlike. However, these patterns may be reversed in some people, while other respondents may not see much difference at all. In other words, there is not any one pattern that is expected here. The point is to simply notice what each side of your brain has to say.

For example, if you checked off items 1 and 2, then perhaps you are struggling with issues related to your self-esteem, especially as it relates to perfectionism. You may think that your work must come out perfectly the first time, and that you must write on a daily basis within a schedule that meets all of your needs—not only as a writer, but as a person. In other words, it's easy for us to imagine the "life of a writer" as some amorphous cloud of bliss, floating high above the rigors of daily life. However, as you proceed through the chapters in this book, you will find that your life as a writer is simply a combination of active choices that you can learn how to make—and still be in sync with the rest of your life's responsibilities.

If you checked off items 3 and 4 in the exercise above, you are probably thinking that making a commitment to being a writer will have catastrophic—or at least highly frustrating—effects on your current lifestyle. Item 5 suggests some possible anxiety, which may come from any number of sources. And, if you checked off 6, you may be afraid to put your toe in the pond of creativity for fear of freshwater sharks who may come back to bite you once again. I have worked with so many writers whose creativity had been stymied by the hypercritical voices of authority figures—or other people from whom these writers had sought approval. However, the most important person who can give you the approval you need to declare yourself a writer is you.

Regardless of your responses to this exercise, you can still move forward in making a commitment to write. As mentioned previously, I have worked with many, many writers who would definitely check off number 6: fear of criticism, rejection, or failure, based on the gossamer memories of previous criticism from others.

I once worked with a client who had *several thousand* references for her dissertation, but still could not bring herself to start writing, for fear that she might have left something out. As we discussed her need to go from exploring other researchers' ideas to expressing her own ideas, Sally revealed that her mother had constantly questioned Sally's ideas, always telling her that she didn't know enough to write simple papers in grade school. Eventually, Sally began to see that her mother's perception of her was holding Sally hostage. As Sally let go of the idea that she didn't have to be perfect, she actually started to write her dissertation—and completed it soon thereafter.

Other clients with whom I have worked have discussed being humiliated at the hands of hypercritical teachers, irascible academic advisors, or disparaging spouses or partners. Most of us have at least one instance of feeling belittled at the hands of someone from whom we'd like to have approval, but we don't have to let them stop us from writing.

A Matter of Commitment

So, without further ado, let's explore just how committed you feel right now in terms of being a writer. On the following Likert scale, circle the number that best represents your current level of commitment to writing. Answer with your dominant hand and then with the other hand. Go with your instinctive response.

	DOMINANT HAND	
NO COMMITMENT	0 1 2 3 4 5 6 7 8 9 10	FULL COMMITMENT

	NONDOMINANT HAND	
NO COMMITMENT	0 1 2 3 4 5 6 7 8 9 10	FULL COMMITMENT

As you peruse your responses, take note: Which side of your brain has been running the show? Which side of your brain would you put in charge of your writing career? When I circled my responses, my dominant hand circled an 8, which reflects my strong commitment to writing—while still having time for the rest of my life. However, my nondominant hand circled a 3, indicating my earlier fears in life about becoming a writer. You can guess which side of my brain is writing this sentence right now.

Let's qualify your answers to the exercise above. After all, what exactly is a 3 in terms of level of commitment? In this next exercise (adapted from Gestalt therapists' focus on language awareness), check off any items that resonate for you, first with your dominant hand and then with your nondominant hand. Feel free to fill in the blanks if any answers come to mind.

DOMINANT HAND
I *should* make a commitment to being a writer.
Reason:
I *need to* make a commitment to being a writer.
Reason:
I *want to* make a commitment to being a writer.
Reason:
I *choose to* make a commitment to being a writer.
Reason:
NONDOMINANT HAND
I *should* make a commitment to being a writer.
Reason:
I *need to* make a commitment to being a writer.
Reason:
I *want to* make a commitment to being a writer.
Reason:
I *choose to* make a commitment to being a writer.
Reason:

Check for trends between the two sets of answers: Is one side of your brain more committed to writing than the other side—and if so, why? Can you feel the difference between saying what you "should" write as opposed to what you "want" or "choose" to write? Generally, people tend to feel more empowered by the time they get to the "choose" option in this kind of exercise.

Perhaps you feel that you *should* write, because you have talent and things to say. Sometimes you may feel that you *need* to write in order to sort out your thoughts or your feelings. Maybe you *want* to write because you enjoy it so much. Taking the next step and declaring that you *choose* to write—because writing is one way to express your true self—is the biggest step of all.

In contrast, you may find that others say you *should not* write, or that you *don't need* to write, because it is a waste of time, or because it doesn't pay the proverbial rent, or because it takes time away from your loved ones. Maybe you even say these things to yourself, and have trouble letting go of these sabotaging thoughts. However, if you still *want* to write, and then *choose* to write, you have started to make a real commitment toward being a writer.

A Matter of Balance

So how do we get past all these negative messages from others—or from within ourselves? One way you can try to do so is by using a bi-vocal technique I call *interior dialogue*, in which the two sides of the brain attempt to communicate and compromise by writing back and forth to each other. If, for example, a compromise must be made between a 3 and a 9, perhaps a 7 can be selected and then implemented into the parameters of your current lifestyle.

Here is a sample of interior dialogue that you can use to help cajole both sides of your brain into working together, rather than against each other. Notice that you need to use your *nondominant* hand to fill in the blanks—with the exception of the second to last item written in bold, for which you use your dominant hand to complete the sentence.

INTERIOR DIALOGUE
DOMINANT HAND: What stops you from making a commitment to being a writer?
NONDOMINANT HAND:
DOMINANT HAND: What would you need in order to get past what's thwarting you?
NONDOMINANT HAND:
DOMINANT HAND: So how can we go about getting that for you?
NONDOMINANT HAND:
DOMINANT HAND: **Okay, so how about if we** _____**?**
NONDOMINANT HAND:

Were you able to allow the two sides of your brain to create a solution that works for you? If not, don't despair—this is only one of many opportunities you'll have in this book to learn how to get what you need as a writer, from both sides of your brain. As a matter of fact, after you have completed the rest of the exercises in this book, you may find it helpful to return to this chapter's interior monologue, and see how you respond then. In my work with clients who are writers, I have found that many of them do know what they need in order to start writing—they just don't know how to get it. Sometimes the simplest response is the best. For example, here's how I responded to this exercise a week ago.

INTERIOR DIALOGUE
DOMINANT HAND: What stops you from making a commitment to being a writer?
NONDOMINANT HAND: *time, or I'm tired, or I want to do something else right now*
DOMINANT HAND: What would you need in order to get past what's thwarting you?
NONDOMINANT HAND: *some energy and fun*
DOMINANT HAND: So how can we go about getting that for you?
NONDOMINANT HAND: *the movies and more energy*
DOMINANT HAND: **Okay, so how about if we** *select a movie for later and get something cold to drink?*
NONDOMINANT HAND: *okay*

These responses are fairly typical of my attitude toward writing now. I know it takes energy to focus, and I know sometimes

I'd rather be out throwing a Frisbee, but I also know that the childlike right side of my brain needs reassurance that fun and energy will indeed be provided. So today, I mixed up a batch of iced tea with orange juice, and I did choose a movie I can see tomorrow with my loved ones. Although writing is enjoyable work, it is also hard work: and the right side of the brain—which is also dominant for activating the "reward" center of the brain—needs to know it will indeed be rewarded for working so hard.

Yes, you are probably saying, but writing is intrinsically rewarding—we get to see the finished product of our labor! However, we also need to balance our hard work with our need for relaxation and leisure time. The brain is like a sponge: it will only absorb so much before it is saturated, and at that point, it needs to be wrung out before it can absorb anything again.

Therefore, part of our commitment to being writers means also making a commitment to live in a balanced way as *human beings who happen to be writers*. All too often, we won't take leisure time because we "haven't written" that day, so we sulk and wish we'd written something that day, and punish ourselves by depriving ourselves of a little fun. However, sometimes it's better to build in the "fun" part first, before we sit down to write. It's just another way of bargaining between the two sides of the brain—another way of adjusting our expectations in order to clarify one aspect of our natural writing rhythms.

The Coaching Versus the Craving Brain

Let's try one more technique to strengthen your resolve about making the commitment to writing. Since the more logical left side of the brain is more like a coach, we need to develop that voice into one of compassion and encouragement. Since the right side of the brain is more like a craving child, we need to coax it into listening to the "coach" just on the other side of the corpus callosum. In this section, we'll explore two ways to facilitate this process.

First, let's take a glance at a few three-letter words that may be essential in establishing your role as a writer: *but, and, yet.* Notice how they affect the following sentences.

1. *I want to write,* but *I haven't written.*
2. *I want to write,* and *I haven't written.*
3. *I haven't written* yet.

Notice how these sentences progress from a stagnant position to a more optimistic attitude about writing. Believe it or not, psychologists have conducted research for decades to study the effects of our thoughts and beliefs on our actions. The result has been a type of therapy known as cognitive-behavioral therapy. One form of this therapy, developed by Dr. Albert Ellis, is called *rational-emotive therapy* (RET). Sounds like a nice blend between the "rational" left brain and the more "emotive" right brain, doesn't it?

Here's how it works. Most of the time, we think that something happens (we get called into work, a child gets sick), and therefore we don't write that day. It's as if the event somehow caused our reaction, right? Well, according to RET, this isn't quite so clear-cut. For example, suppose a snake enters the room—what would you do? Like many people, you'd probably hop up on a chair or table to get away from the snake while you decide what to do. However, suppose a toddler sees this snake before you do, and the toddler goes over to the snake to touch it. How is it that the same snake has you jumping on a table and a toddler petting it?

The reality is that it's not the snake that's causing your—or the toddler's—behavior. It's what you and the toddler *believe* about the snake that causes your divergent reactions. Here's how this would look in a traditional RET paradigm.

A = Activating Event:	*Snake comes into the room.*
B = Belief:	YOU: That snake is dangerous.
	KID: That's a pretty toy.
C = Consequences:	YOU: Jump up on chair (fear).
	KID: Go play with snake (curiosity).

At first glance, it may seem that we are at the mercy of our thoughts or beliefs. However, we don't have to be held hostage by our beliefs, because we are capable of changing them. That's where the second part of this approach comes in handy. After A, B, and C comes D—actively disputing and challenging our beliefs—and E—the effects of these challenges to our own way of thinking. One could say that with this approach, the left brain is more in charge here, although the right brain will experience the emotional effects of the left brain's logical thought process.

Let's see how this could play out with the previous example, and then we'll apply it to the writing process.

A = Activating Event:	*Snake comes into the room.*
B = Belief:	YOU: That snake is dangerous.
	KID: That's a pretty toy.
C = Consequences:	YOU: Jump up on chair (fear).
	KID: Go play with snake (curiosity).

D = Dispute (Dispute and disagree with your beliefs):
YOU: Maybe the snake isn't dangerous.
KID: Maybe this snake isn't safe to play with.

E = (Effects of changing your beliefs):
YOU: I can drop a wastebasket over it, then call for help.
KID: I should ask a grown-up if this is okay to play with.

As you can see, changing the belief changes the outcome in both cases. So let's apply this technique to the writing process.

A = Activating Event:	*Friend says my writing is "a pipe dream."*
B = Belief:	They're right—I'm an imposter.
C = Consequences:	I feel incompetent. I stop writing.

D = Dispute (Dispute and disagree with your beliefs):
Wait, I do still want to write. I have something to say.

E = (Effects of changing your beliefs):
EMOTION: I feel calmer now.
THOUGHT: My writing is important to me, and that's enough.
BEHAVIOR: I'll continue to write.

Again, as you can see, when we target our *beliefs*, we can challenge them, and change the way we *feel* (right brain), the way we *think* (left brain), and the way we *behave* in response to any situation that could thwart our efforts at writing.

For example, I've worked with many clients who wouldn't allow themselves to embrace the notion of being writers for fear they'd outshine others. Here's how one of those cases might play out in this RET format.

A = Activating Event:	*Mother always wanted to be a writer.*
B = Belief:	She might get jealous and she'll feel bad.
C = Consequences:	I can't outshine her. I won't write.

D = Dispute (Dispute and disagree with your own beliefs):
But I do want to write. She didn't have the opportunities that I do. She raised five children during the Depression, no less. Maybe I'll dedicate my book to my mother.

E = (Effects of changing your own beliefs):
EMOTION: I feel fine about this now.
THOUGHT: She always says she wants what's best for me.
BEHAVIOR: I'll start to write.

Now, let's try one that seems relevant for you. Fill in the blanks for A and C. Then go back and try to determine what your Beliefs are. Then move on to D and E from there.

RATIONAL-EMOTIVE THERAPY
A = ACTIVATING EVENT:
B = BELIEF:
C = CONSEQUENCES:
D = DISPUTE (DISPUTE AND DISAGREE WITH YOUR BELIEFS):
E = (EFFECTS OF CHANGING YOUR BELIEFS):
EMOTION:
THOUGHT:
BEHAVIOR:

As you peruse your responses, notice the feeling of empowerment that you can attain not only from becoming aware of your self-defeating beliefs, but also from actively challenging these beliefs in order to change the way you feel, think, and react to obstacles regarding your role as a writer. In other words, you can do this any time you feel stuck in your role as a writer as well as throughout any part of the writing process.

Your Declaration of Independence

You may be asking yourself why you haven't done this before, or perhaps why you haven't ever given yourself permission to challenge your inner beliefs and the discouraging comments of others. Well, now is as good a time as any. Today, if you so choose, you may declare your independence from what I call "writer's identity block."

This may not be a binding legal document—although I suppose you could get it notarized—but it's close enough to fool the right side of your brain. So, without further ado, see if you feel like signing the following contract. Be sure to select your witness carefully—someone who is truly supportive of you and your role as a writer. Feel better?

OFFICIAL DECLARATION OF INDEPENDENCE FROM WRITER'S IDENTITY BLOCK

I, _____, hereby declare that I am making a commitment to allow myself to become a writer and to call myself a "writer."

Signed:

YOUR NAME	*WITNESS*
DATE	*DATE*

To Do or Not To Do List

You've made the commitment. Now what can you do to help ensure that this time, it sticks? Well, if you're like most people, you probably think you need some kind of to-do list, even though you may actually detest to-do lists. On the one hand, these lists can be reassuring, since what you need to do is finally written down so you won't forget it. On the other hand, a to-do list expects to be done. It's as if it has a life of its own, like some tyrant demanding that we accomplish these tasks. This reaction is usually emanating from the right side of your brain—the Craving Brain that just wants to have fun.

Well, have you ever tried to get toddlers to the dinner table? They usually don't like that. This is in part because you are interrupting their fun—by definition they wouldn't be engaging in the activity if it wasn't fun—and in part because toddlers are striving so hard for independence that the word "no" becomes their mantra. One way out of this dilemma is to give the child a perception of choice: "Do you want to come to dinner in one minute or five minutes?" Of course, the child goes for five minutes, whether she has developed a concept of time or not, because it sounds like "more." And so it goes for the childlike right side of the brain.

That's why I like to call my lists by a different name. Since the right brain has to feel that it has some choice in the matter, I call this the "To Do or Not To Do List" (with apologies to Mr. Shakespeare). You can choose to do these tasks, or not do them. (Honestly, there's no quiz.)

So here is your list for moving forward on what you've learned in this chapter. Feel free to add or delete items as you wish.

1. Call someone who cares and tell him or her I am a writer.
2. Buy colored folders, binders, pens, bins, etc. to give my musings a home.
3. Decide to read next chapter of this book.

As you check off these items—or not—in this list, remember: It's all about choice. And the choice is yours.

CHAPTER 3

Hyped or Mellow?

It's my experience that very few writers, young or old, are really seeking advice when they give out their work to be read. They want support; they want someone to say, "Good job."

JOHN IRVING

Writing is the hardest work in the world not involving heavy lifting.

PETER HAMILL

That Elusive Writing Mood

"I have to be in the mood to write," said Sam, a nurse and would-be novelist. Like many of my other clients, Sam was tyrannized by this "high-energy" myth that plagues authors everywhere. If you are a full-time writer, then you may have the luxury of waiting until the Muse drops by with a bucket of Starbucks' best. However, if you're like Sam—a person with a full-time job, family, and other responsibilities—waiting for an ultimately energized Muse can become a frustrating endeavor.

Before getting married, Sam had so much free time that he had the luxury of waiting until the mood to write struck him. Now that his life's circumstances had changed, he could no longer jazz himself up on caffeine and cigarettes to "get pumped up for writing." He had quit smoking once he'd had children, and couldn't afford crabby caffeine hangovers, if only for the sake of his toddler twins. Eventually, I was able to help him see that he had choices besides coffee and cigarettes to start the writing process. He learned how to *choose* his mood when it came to writing.

Like so many other writers, I have struggled with this same dilemma. I used to feel like I had to have all neurons firing at lightning speed before I could even pick up a pen. Psychologists might call this "hypomania," which falls below the full criteria for an actual manic episode. In other words, you haven't hopped on a solo flight to Paris on a whim. Rather, you may just need to feel like you're sitting on the edge of your seat with creative flashes constantly whizzing through your brain.

Alternatively, I have worked with a number of writers who felt too "hyped up" to write. One client, Duncan, became so anxious whenever he needed to write that he couldn't even get himself to sit down in order to write. He'd pace his apartment, looking for other things to do, all the while berating himself for not writing, and then end up accomplishing nothing at all, other than raising his level of anxiety. Eventually, he'd end up making friends with Ben & Jerry again, and their distant cousins, potato chips and dip—all of which increase levels of calming neurotransmitters and hormones such as serotonin and endorphins.

Like so many people, Duncan had grown up in a household filled with constant turmoil. His central nervous system had become acclimated to the high-intensity mood generated by such chaos, so he really only felt "normal" when he was anxious. He knew, however, that such anxiety threw him into a tailspin when it came to writing. He realized that this feeling of being on guard for the next fiasco was an effective coping skill during his childhood, but now this feeling no longer served him. He now lived alone in a placid household, and began to realize that he needn't be on guard anymore. He was able to learn new ways of reducing his nervous energy (a few yoga poses, some relaxing herbal tea), and decided that writing in the rich silence of the local library was a good choice for him.

I have also worked with many clients who would just go numb at the thought of writing. They would simply stare at the desk, the blank page, the blinking cursor—as if they were frozen. One client, a biologist I'll call Jane, exhibited this classic "freeze response" whenever she tried to work on her master's thesis. Researchers have found—in both animals and humans—that this freeze response, just like the fight-or-flight response, may occur when there is a threat. We freeze up or "play dead," just like a reptile might, in order to avoid being attacked by a predator. As a biologist, Jane understood the concept of the freeze response. But who or what was her predator?

In Jane's case, as with many writers, the predator was actually the ghost of rejections past. Jane had grown up with well-meaning but perfectionist parents, so of course she had learned that perfection was the only option, regardless of the task. When it came to writing her thesis, she would freeze up in the same way she used to whenever her parents would verbally harangue her for not getting all As, not making the cheerleaders' team, not being thin enough—you name it.

As Jane began to understand that her body was simply reenacting that old childhood feeling of shame, she also began to see that she could never have been "perfect enough" for her parents, and she didn't have to be perfect for her thesis committee members, either. She realized that her parents had meant well, but they had projected their own feelings of inadequacy onto her—and she was not responsible for their desire for perfection.

Similarly, she realized that she had been assuming that her thesis committee members would be hypercritical, and that would mean she'd never please them, and therefore never finish the paper, and never graduate—so why bother? But as Jane began to view her professors as human beings, not just scholars, she could see that they simply wanted her to do her best work. That's why they were there, to guide her.

Of course, as is often the case, one of her thesis committee members was a bit gruff and held extremely high expectations of Jane. Yet she was able to see that this had nothing to do with her, and everything to do with the professor. Other students had lamented his rigid standards, and Jane was able to see that she didn't have to take his demanding academic demeanor personally. He was just there to give suggestions, and she knew her ultimate answers would come from her thesis advisor, who had privately admitted to Jane that, yes, this other committee member was well-known for raising the academic bar whenever possible.

Once Jane saw that she didn't have to repeat the past by "playing dead" whenever she was evaluated, she worked steadily on her thesis. Additionally, Jane soon found that surrounding herself with an aesthetically pleasing environment (her home office) was a way in which she could feel more comfortable during the writing process—because this was a zone she had created for herself, with only her own standards in mind. She even followed my suggestion to hang a small framed photo so that it was slightly crooked—as a reminder that she didn't have to live up to anyone's perfectionistic standards! As a result, Jane could relax in this environment of her own creation and eventually completed her thesis.

However, I've also seen numerous clients who felt they wrote best when they could write in an environment bustling with activity: airports, restaurants, you name it. It was as if the busy environment could help these writers reinforce and maintain their energized states (although other writers may find this kind of environment quite draining). It certainly used to work for me, but at what cost to my adrenal glands? Now that I've found some ways to balance my health with my writing needs, I'd say my stress response system is a lot happier that I choose a quiet café if I feel the need to write away from home on any given day.

Let's see how you feel about the amount of energy you feel you need in order to write. Try to fill in the blank lines below with your first, gut-instinct answers.

DOMINANT HAND
When I think of the level of energy I need to write, I think:
When I think of the level of energy I need to write, I feel:

NONDOMINANT HAND
When I think of the level of energy I need to write, I think:
When I think of the level of energy I need to write, I feel:

Do you notice similarities or differences between your responses? Do your answers surprise you, or do they express what you already know about yourself as a writer? How do you feel about your responses? Here are my responses to this exercise.

DOMINANT HAND
When I think of the level of energy I need to write, I think:
I'm not twenty-nine anymore!
When I think of the level of energy I need to write, I feel:
okay, because I can tune my energy to the stage of the writing process I can do at any given time (e.g., jotting down ideas versus creating sentences/paragraphs)
NONDOMINANT HAND
When I think of the level of energy I need to write, I think:
I have to be wide awake
When I think of the level of energy I need to write, I feel:
sometimes I'm too tired

These answers don't surprise me. Although my logical left brain recognizes the limitations of my age, my right brain still wants to be wide awake (a.k.a., practically hypomanic). The right side of the brain is more closely connected to the limbic system, the primitive part of the brain that focuses on survival. Accordingly, the right side of the brain is dominant for triggering the classic fight-or-flight response. Having had my own bouts with writer's block, I have taken the liberty of dubbing this the *write-or-flight* response. In other words, we can sit down and write with our adrenal glands loaded and ready for action, or fly off into cyberspace, into our cars headed for the nearest caffeine outlet, or perhaps just into the kitchen to scrub countertops or balance the checkbook—any meaningless activity will do. This helps to dissipate the anxiety inherent in the write-or-flight response, but it usually means we don't get any writing done whatsoever.

Many of my clients have struggled with this vortex of meaningless activity as an alternative to writing. For example, one client, Melissa, used to clean her entire kitchen so that she would have room to write on the dining room table, the surface of which she hadn't seen in years. This endeavor to clear the decks would entail rummaging through piles of bills, receipts, pieces of short stories, and anything else she could fit on what she hoped was still her dining room table. Additionally, she'd feel compelled to clean all countertops in the adjoining kitchen area, organize her latest (and earliest) recipe clippings from her favorite magazine, mop the floor, and of course pitch any unintended science projects from the refrigerator. These tasks would all be done in no particular order—just whatever grabbed her attention at any given moment. Usually, she would multitask and do several, if not all, of these tasks simultaneously.

And the end result? A sparkling kitchen that would impress Martha Stewart, a dining room table sleek with Lemon Pledge, and one deflated writer who could have accomplished all of these tasks piecemeal throughout the week. At this point, Melissa either would be too tired to write or would have simply used up the time allotted for writing that day. However, once she began to work with some of the exercises in this book as part of her therapy with me, she was well on the way to not only understanding but actually changing the underlying thought process that triggered her write-or-flight response.

Let's take a closer look at some of the reasons behind this write-or-flight response. The items below pertain to our levels of energy when we are writing. Check off any items that apply to you, and feel free to fill in the blanks as you see fit.

	DOMINANT HAND
	1. If I feel relaxed, I am more likely to write.
	2. I have to be totally energized to write anything at all.
	3. I have to be in the mood to write.
	4. I know the best time of day for me, in terms of my mood, is at _____, but I can't write then because _____.
	5. If I wrote when I was in the mood, _____ would be upset.
	6. If I stand up for myself and insist on writing when I'm in the mood, then _____ might react by _____.
	NONDOMINANT HAND
	1. If I feel relaxed, I am more likely to write.
	2. I have to be totally energized to write anything at all.
	3. I have to be in the mood to write.
	4. I know the best time of day for me, in terms of my mood, is at _____, but I can't write then because _____.
	5. If I wrote when I was in the mood, _____ would be upset.
	6. If I stand up for myself and insist on writing when I'm in the mood, then _____ might react by _____.

Now, take a look at your responses. Do they pertain strictly to you (items 1 through 3), or do others affect your decision about when to write (items 4 through 6)? How do you feel about your answers? Is there anything you'd like to change about your natural rhythms in terms of your preferred "writing mood"? Perhaps your answers are divergent, or at the very least, confusing.

For example, in working with Rita, I could see that she felt conflicted about the writing mood she'd been craving for years. She said that she was most alert midmorning and therefore preferred to write at 10 A.M., but couldn't because of her shift at the hospital. As a nurse, she just couldn't imagine taking time away from patients on her floor at precisely 10:00 each day. Instead, Rita decided to pick the second best time for her to write—after work, at about 6:00 P.M. However, Rita felt that in order to write, she needed to be totally relaxed and totally energized at the same time. She knew that this feeling of being on "red alert" while simultaneously remaining calm in a crisis situation served her well as an emergency room nurse. "It makes me feel alive," she said—but it wasn't exactly the right mood for her when she wanted to create poetry. As Rita began to acknowledge that adrenaline wasn't the best fuel for writing poetry, she was able to monitor her energy and mood states in order to create the flow of ideas she had so long wanted to release.

Understanding the Write-or-Flight Response

On the other hand, the idea of being totally relaxed and totally energized at the same time may not be so crazy after all. Dr. Robert Thayer, a psychologist who has conducted research on the nature of stress and tension, has found that, in general, there are four mood states that can be identified. As Dr. Thayer discusses in his books, *The Origin of Everyday Moods* and *Calm-Energy*, one of these mood states—"calm-energy"—is the ideal state for motivation. Here is a list of well-known people who might best illustrate these four mood states.

> *Tense-tired:* Roseanne Barr (Queen of the "leave-me-alone" syndrome)
> *Tense-energy:* Robin Williams (King of the "I-can't-stop-myself-from-bouncing-off-the-walls" syndrome)
> *Calm-energy:* Dalai Lama (Emperor of the "let-it-flow-and-you-shall-be-mellow" syndrome)
> *Calm-tired:* Bill Murray (Prince of the "I'm-so-mellow-I-could-die" syndrome)

Can you guess which moods dominate most of your life? In our society, it's quite common to wake up tense-tired, blast ourselves into tense-energy via caffeine, cigarettes, or whatever the traffic will bear, and then crash back into tense-tired once the day is done. No Dalai Lama here! And forget that calm-tired mood for evening reading in a bubble bath or Jacuzzi; we're too tense-tired to bother with all that. This usually means that we awaken less rested the next day, and it's onto that hamster-cage treadmill from there.

There are many reasons why we might get stuck in one mood, or catapult from one extreme to another. For example, research- ers such as Dr. Allan Schore have found that children who grow up with insecure attachments to their caregivers are more likely to exhibit the following traits:

1. Extremely high or extremely low levels of arousal in the central nervous system
2. Distracted attention
3. Negative emotions

All of these characteristics may engender later difficulties with motivation, concentration, and self-regulation of mood states.

So, you might ask, what makes for an insecure attachment style? Well, basically, having parents and caretakers who were having a life—problems with stress, financial instability, alcohol/ drugs, divorce, unresolved trauma from war experiences or childhood maltreatment, chronic illness, or death—in other words, the human condition. Any of these issues might prevent a caretaker from providing the appropriate levels of affection, gentle guidance, and consistent parenting that all children need to feel securely attached. Even having several children under the age of five at the same time can make a parent less available to a toddler or infant.

Well, I don't know about you, but my family wasn't exactly nestled in next door to The Brady Bunch. And Donna Reed never stopped by to lend a hand, either. As for good old Andy Griffith? Gone fishin'.

Honestly, how many people do you know who grew up in a well-balanced, healthy, relatively problem-free family? For the few who did, they would be most likely to grow up with a secure attachment bond with their caregivers. Accordingly, these chosen few would be expected to exhibit characteristics that correlate with a secure attachment style:

1. Moderate and balanced levels of arousal in the central nervous system
2. Focused attention
3. Positive emotions

All of these characteristics are likely to engender a nicely balanced mood state for task accomplishment.*

Of course, regardless of the levels of chronic stress or lack of emotional support any of us may have experienced as children, as adults we can now learn how to effectively manage our moods and energy levels (see my previous book, *Write*, for a thorough discussion of this process). For example, Dr. Thayer has found that walking briskly for five minutes will increase energy for one and a half hours. We can ditch the coffee for green tea (which creates more energy and less tension), learn how to do a few quick yoga moves (increases energy and reduces tension), and just plain eat well and exercise routinely. *However, please note that if you have been diagnosed with conditions such as attention-deficit/hyperactivity disorder, obsessive-compulsive disorder, panic attacks, generalized anxiety disorder, post-traumatic stress disorder, depression, bipolar disorder, or any other type of mood disorder, it is crucial that you meet with a qualified psychiatrist to determine whether herbal remedies could be harmful and/or whether psychotropic medication is warranted to help you regulate your moods and energy levels.*

---

*See articles by Anke Karl and Astrid Berg in the reference section for further information regarding chronic stress, attachment formation, and brain development.

The Six Mood-Dependent Stages of Writing

There is yet another way to manage the writing process in terms of your moods. We tend to think of writing as a *product*, rather than as a *process*. All too often we count our progress in terms of pages written, rather than in terms of how much time we put into the writing process. If a writing task will take 100 hours, then it doesn't matter how many pages we might create on any given Tuesday—what matters is that the time gets put in, and after approximately 100 hours, the writing project will be completed.

However, the reality is that there are steps in the process of writing. Most of the time, we think of prewriting, writing, and rewriting. I've added three other steps because we do them all anyway and might as well get credit for time served.

Read-writing: Reading what you've already written, or reading something similar to what you'd like to write.

Co-writing: Calling up a friend, colleague, or another writer, and discussing what you want to write, or have written, to get feedback and encouragement (it helps if the other person writes down what you're saying—what comes out is the outline, more or less, for your writing project).

Rote-writing: Typing up lists, references, and anything that doesn't require the mental acuity needed for actual writing—includes typing in handwritten revisions.

Prewriting: Gathering notes, ideas, and resources, and jotting down ideas or outlines.

Writing: Creating sentences, paragraphs, lines of poetry, etc.

Rewriting: Editing, revising.

Each of these stages of writing requires a different level of focus, concentration, and mental energy. What I find most helpful is to match my energy level with one of these six stages of writing. For example, today, I was hovering somewhere between a calm-energy and tense-energy mood, so I decided to write sentences and paragraphs from some notes I'd written a month or so ago for this chapter. In contrast, yesterday I had slipped below the level of tense-tired into a state of zombielike awareness that I was at least still breathing, so I simply typed up some of the exercises and pasted them into various chapters of this book—rote-writing at its very best.

The point is, all of these tasks had to be done at some point, but I no longer force myself to do them in order (at least I won't until I'm revising the entire manuscript).

By matching your moods to these six stages of the writing process, you can begin to get a writing project started—or completed—*without guilt*. You no longer have to berate yourself with the old standby "I've been sitting here for two hours, and I haven't even started *writing* yet." Even if you are simply co-writing, you have already started the writing process. Writing sentences or lines of poetry is only one step out of six possible types of activity that need to be done before you complete a writing project—so pick the one that your energy level will allow you to tackle (or tolerate) at any given time.

And by all means start with the easiest task you can find. Remember—it takes a certain amount of time to complete a writing task, and (at least up until the final revision) it often doesn't matter which part of the writing project you do first. In helping writers who are stymied, I usually ask, "Where exactly are you stuck?" Then I tell them to step away from that part of the writing project and pick something that is more appealing. Usually, after they have gained some momentum by accomplishing a simpler part of the writing task, these writers find the more difficult task they'd abandoned earlier somehow easier to face.

The Eccentric Artist Within

Let's look more closely at your natural expectations about the level of energy you think you need in order to write. Circle the number on the Likert scale below that seems to resonate with you, first with your dominant hand and then with the other hand. Go with your first instinctive response.

DOMINANT HAND												
ASLEEP	0	1	2	3	4	5	6	7	8	9	10	HYPER-ENERGIZED

NONDOMINANT HAND												
ASLEEP	0	1	2	3	4	5	6	7	8	9	10	HYPER-ENERGIZED

Now that you have calibrated your naturally occurring rhythms, do you feel surprised? Which side of your brain is dictating your writing mood? Would you like to change that, or reach a compromise of sorts?

With my dominant hand, I circled numbers 5 and 6—which is usually what I prefer if I am actually writing sentences and paragraphs. If my energy is at a 3 or 4, I'm more likely to do some rote-writing. If I'm at a 2 or below, then co-writing with a fellow writer is my best option.

However, with my nondominant hand, I circled numbers 9 and 10—my right brain's vote for that intense energy (caffeine-induced, of course) that more often than not will catapult me into the write-or-flight response in a heartbeat (pun intended). And guess which option I usually choose? In other words, although the Eccentric Artist Within hates to admit it, I know that moderation is the best policy for generating my writing moods. I can sip a cup of green tea, instead of a vat of espresso, and eat some high-protein foods along with a few pieces of dark chocolate—and that suits me just fine nowadays.

Let's see if you can make some compromises by getting votes from both sides of your brain. Respond to the items in the next exercise that resonate with you by filling in the energy level (anywhere from 0 to 10). Feel free to add reasons as you see fit.

Note how you feel as you peruse your responses: Are you pleasantly surprised, a bit agitated, or perhaps somewhere in between? Were you able to choose an energy level that feels right for you in your current life situation? Perhaps you'd prefer an energy level of 8 because that feels just right for you.

DOMINANT HAND
I *should* have an energy level of ___ when I write.
Reason:
I *need to* have an energy level of ___ when I write.
Reason:
I *want to* have an energy level of ___ when I write.
Reason:
I *choose to* have an energy level of ___ when I write.
Reason:

NONDOMINANT HAND
I *should* have an energy level of ___ when I write.
Reason:
I *need to* have an energy level of ___ when I write.
Reason:
I *want to* have an energy level of ___ when I write.
Reason:
I *choose to* have an energy level of ___ when I write.
Reason:

However, maybe you can actually write with an energy level of 4, depending on the stage of the writing process you choose. Of course, if you're anything like me, the more demanding, childlike right brain may still crave the excitement of an energy level of 10. In spite of that, however, I have learned how to write effectively—by engaging in one of the six writing stages mentioned earlier—regardless of my energy level. And I have learned that a 10 isn't really the best option for me.

If you found that your responses are conflicting, and you still can't find a compromise, try the interior dialogue below. Allow the two sides of your brain to converse so that you can make some helpful choices about your moods and energy levels during the writing process.

INTERIOR DIALOGUE
DOMINANT HAND: What stops you from effectively managing your energy level for the writing process?
NONDOMINANT HAND:
DOMINANT HAND: What would you need in order to get past what's thwarting you?
NONDOMINANT HAND:
DOMINANT HAND: So how can we go about getting that for you?
NONDOMINANT HAND:
DOMINANT HAND: **Okay, so how about if we** _____**?**
NONDOMINANT HAND:

As you examine your answers, ask yourself whether they resonate with what you feel you need. Were you able to set up a compromise to help establish the appropriate level of energy you need in order to write? If so, great. If not, there's no need to worry about it. The exercises in the next few chapters may offer you more insight—and flexibility—in terms of managing your mood and energy for the writing process.

Here are my answers to this exercise.

INTERIOR DIALOGUE
DOMINANT HAND: What stops you from effectively managing your energy level for the writing process?
NONDOMINANT HAND: *I get confused and mad*
DOMINANT HAND: What would you need in order to get past what's thwarting you?
NONDOMINANT HAND: *some more energy*
DOMINANT HAND: So how can we go about getting that for you?
NONDOMINANT HAND: *I don't know, maybe some candy*
DOMINANT HAND: **Okay, so how about if we** *have a bit of dark chocolate and then only write the parts or kind of stuff we have energy for***?**
NONDOMINANT HAND: *good*

My childlike right brain gets confused (how do I do this?) and mad (as in frustrated, no sense of control). Sure, I would like to have more energy, but how? Well, candy, of course! I can also see that my reassuring left brain talks back using diction that any kid can understand: "parts of" or "kind of stuff" (instead of listing the six writing stages mentioned above, which could be overwhelming for a child). Fortunately, after all these years of listening to both sides of my brain, I can usually come up with some kind of compromise that allows me to engage in the writing process.

Let's challenge some of our beliefs about the writing process. Let's take the case of Jack, who felt frustrated about trying to get in that elusive writing mood, so he just stopped writing. As we discussed his reasons for avoiding writing, the truth began to unravel. Here is how his RET chart would look.

A = Activating Event: *I'm not in the mood to write. I'm too tired.*

B = Belief: I have no control over my mood.

C = Consequences: I feel frustrated and angry.

D = Dispute (Dispute and disagree with your own beliefs):
But I still like to write. I could try a brisk five-minute walk, have tea, do deep breathing, or go to the gym and ride the bike for a half hour. Or, I could edit what I wrote last week, or type references.

E = (Effects of changing your own beliefs):
EMOTION: I feel more in charge now.
THOUGHT: I can change my mood, or change what I'm working on.
BEHAVIOR: I'll write for an hour, then watch T.V.

As you can see, changing the belief changes the outcome. So, let's apply this technique to your experience with the writing process. (Again, just use your dominant hand for this exercise.) First, fill in the blanks for A and C. Then go back and try to determine what your Beliefs are. Then fill out sections D and E.

RATIONAL-EMOTIVE THERAPY
A = ACTIVATING EVENT:
B = BELIEF:
C = CONSEQUENCES:
D = DISPUTE (DISPUTE AND DISAGREE WITH YOUR BELIEFS):
E = (EFFECTS OF CHANGING YOUR BELIEFS):
EMOTION:
THOUGHT:
BEHAVIOR:

As you peruse your responses, notice any feelings, especially about the thought of being more in control of your life. Keep in mind that you can use this technique any time you feel like you're just "not in the mood" to write.

Here is your list for moving forward on what you've learned in this chapter. Just check off the items that resonate with you as a writer.

	TO DO OR NOT TO DO LIST
	1. Call someone who cares and tell him or her about your writing moods.
	2. Buy something that will help to energize you or calm you, as needed: yoga mat or book, herbal tea, your favorite proteins (such as lean meats, low-fat dairy products), perhaps some dark chocolate.
	3. Keep a list of the six stages of the writing process with you at all times, so you can remind yourself that you can "write" no matter what mood you're in.
	4. Select a chair for a twenty-minute "power nap" (take before 5:00 P.M. to avoid disrupting sleep patterns) to get your mind ready for writing.
	5. Decide to read the next chapter in this book.

And of course, give yourself permission to do some leisure activities for which you might be in the mood: As the old saying goes, all work and no play keeps your writing at bay . . .

CHAPTER 4

Organized or Chaotic?

I put things down on sheets of paper and
stuff them in my pockets. When I have
enough, I have a book.

JOHN LENNON

I keep a small sheath of 3 × 5 cards in my billfold. If
I think of a good sentence, I'll write it down . . . Of
course, when I come back to it, the line may change
considerably. Occasionally, there's one that sings so
perfectly the first time that it stays, like, *My boy has
stopped speaking to me and I don't think I can bear
it.* I wrote that down on a 3 × 5 card, perhaps on a
bus, or after walking the dog. I store them in filing
cabinets. The file on *Something Happened* is about
four inches deep, the one on *Catch-22* about the
length of a shoebox.

JOSEPH HELLER

Papers, Papers Everywhere

Many writers are held hostage by the dual tyrants of clutter and chaos. The result? Echoes from *The Rime of the Ancient Mariner* (with apologies to Samuel Taylor Coleridge): papers, papers everywhere—and not one of them filled with our poems, essays, short stories, novel scenes, or dissertation chapters. Instead, there are piles of bills, receipts, miscellaneous "important" papers, and newspaper clippings strewn across our desks. Just the sight of all this chaos can trigger the write-or-flight response for us, to the point where we avoid our writing area at all costs. Sound familiar?

I am reminded of one client, Emma, whom I helped to understand the nature of the clutter that had plagued her for many years. She was just beginning to see that the sight of clutter can easily trigger negative emotions in the visually dominant right side of the brain. She would come home from her job as a waitress, thinking once again that perhaps she'd attempt to work on her novel that night. However, the very first thing she'd see upon opening her apartment door was this: a set of shelves jammed with a hodgepodge of books and magazines; a kitchen table adorned with everything from unopened junk mail to unreturned phone messages; and, off to the right, her desk covered with a chaotic jumble of half-written scenes, numerous outlines, a cracked mug with a one-inch layer of calcified coffee, and a pile of hand-washables waiting to be rescued from oblivion.

When I asked Emma what she first thought upon entering her home, she said, "What a mess—I have to get out of here." I then asked her what she was *feeling* when she opened the door to all this clutter and disorganization, and she said, "I feel lost, empty, and overwhelmed." Then she added this: "It keeps me feeling bad, so I can't move forward in my life. I can't write until I clean up my writing area, and I don't ever get it organized, so I just end up holding myself back."

Although Emma had a degree—and talent—in creative writing, she was indeed holding herself back. Upon further exploration, when I asked Emma if she could recall an earlier time when she'd felt "lost, empty, and overwhelmed," her eyes brimmed with tears. She then told me how distressed she would feel at age eight, coming home to a disorganized and cluttered home with her alcoholic mother passed out on the couch. Emma felt lost because she had no one to turn to for help with her school project; empty because, for her, the house was devoid of human contact; and overwhelmed because she felt simultaneously responsible and helpless regarding the unending chaos of her surroundings.

According to experts such as Eliana Gil, author of *Outgrowing the Pain*, most of us will gravitate toward the familiar (rather than unfamiliar)—even if it isn't healthy for us. For Emma, keeping herself trapped by clutter was one way of keeping the "legacy" of her mother, who had died when Emma was nineteen.

However, Emma began to see that she no longer needed to replicate the familiar but unhealthy conditions of her childhood home, and she began to embrace the right-brain organizational strategies I had offered months earlier—before she was ready to let go of her patterns of chaotic living. Soon after, she began working steadily on her novel—and enjoying the process, no less!

I have worked with some writers who have brought in photographs of their chaotic writing zones. One in particular stands out in my mind. Martin, a senior analyst at a research firm, was a divorced man living in his new apartment. What was most remarkable, upon closer scrutiny of his photographs of his writing room, was the layout of his clutter. Martin usually sat in the same easy chair whether he was eating dinner, watching TV, or talking on the phone. When he looked off to the right of his favorite chair (the logical left brain's view), the room was relatively organized. However, when he looked off to the left of his chair (the chaotic right brain's view), the picture was decidedly different: papers, books, unwrapped holiday gifts, magazines, and other items in dire need of homes. When Martin saw that he had created two different zones in his writing area—one Spartan, the other a jumble of "treasures"—he could see the struggle between the two sides of his brain and began to unravel some of the mystery behind his writer's block.

Like so many people, Martin had been raised by parents who may have meant well but who engaged in flawed parenting. Although Martin would allow his taskmaster father to believe that he had finished his grade-school homework in the time allotted, this wasn't the whole truth. After supposedly completing his school work, Martin was permitted to explore his favorite books, toys, and the great outdoors of his large backyard.

However, Martin would actually finish his homework after he'd gone to bed—with a flashlight as his study guide. This had offered him some semblance of control, but it also kept him sleep-deprived and in constant dread of being caught by his father. And this pattern clearly reflected the dichotomy between his "obedient," logical left brain and his "rebellious," emotional right brain—to the point where the arrangement of the clutter in his room reflected these two choices!

Creating Order out of Chaos

Let's examine which side of your brain is unable to create order out of chaos. See what comes up when you respond to this parallel monologue.

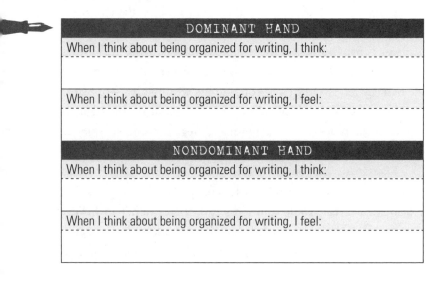

DOMINANT HAND

When I think about being organized for writing, I think:

When I think about being organized for writing, I feel:

NONDOMINANT HAND

When I think about being organized for writing, I think:

When I think about being organized for writing, I feel:

As you review your answers, look for patterns. Maybe you're startled by one or more of your responses, or perhaps this is familiar territory for you.

My responses to this parallel monologue reveal some of the conflict I have within myself about how I "should" organize my writing area.

DOMINANT HAND
When I think about being organized for writing, I think:
it's hard to keep it all looking neat
When I think about being organized for writing, I feel:
frustrated
NONDOMINANT HAND
When I think about being organized for writing, I think:
who cares?
When I think about being organized for writing, I feel:
bored

It's clear that the left side of my brain knows that keeping things in order is difficult, even though I try. However, my right brain doesn't really care if things are neat and tidy, let alone organized—it's too boring. This sounds reminiscent of what any child might say if you asked him to clean up his bedroom. Why would a kid want to do that? It's just not fun, and therefore not relevant.

Let's examine this issue more closely, and see what the two sides of your brain have to say about all this. Check off any items below that seem accurate for you, first with your dominant hand and then with your nondominant hand.

DOMINANT HAND
1. I get overwhelmed just looking at my writing area/desk.
2. I can't stand the thought of organizing all my notes.
3. I don't have time to set up a writing "nest."
4. I can't imagine having a writing area that would work for me.
5. I prefer to pile, rather than to file.
6. If I get organized, I'm afraid I still won't write anything.

NONDOMINANT HAND
1. I get overwhelmed just looking at my writing area/desk.
2. I can't stand the thought of organizing all my notes.
3. I don't have time to set up a writing "nest."
4. I can't imagine having a writing area that would work for me.
5. I prefer to pile, rather than to file.
6. If I get organized, I'm afraid I still won't write anything.

Check your answers: Do they surprise you, or not? Can you spot trends that offer clues as to why you might struggle with organizing your writing area?

Most writers check off number 5. If you are more of a visual person, then of course you would prefer to pile rather than to file. After all, once something is filed, if you can't see it, it doesn't exist, right? And even if you could let your logical left brain convince you to file things, you'd probably still struggle with how to categorize things "perfectly."

At some point I just create a general category, even if it's "Misc. stuff for novel #1" or "Misc. stuff for novel #2" or "Misc. stuff for jacket cover of book." Most importantly, it's off of my desk so I have room to write. I can always further subcategorize these big files later. Another approach to clearing off your desk is to simply place the piles in colored boxes or colored gusseted files with stickers labeled in terms of where the piles were on the desk: *Upper Left Corner, Upper Middle of Desk, Upper Right Corner,* and so on—more about this later.

In response to this same exercise, you most likely endorsed other items than just number 5, perhaps with conflicting responses. For example, I did this exercise today, and with my nondominant hand, I checked off all the items with the exception of number 3: for some reason, the right side of my brain isn't concerned about having enough *time* to set up a writing nest, but my right brain does know what it wants. This makes sense to me, since the right side of the brain is dominant for sensory input. I do enjoy visualizing a beautiful writing area, with all of my favorite colors and a Spartan desk with just the right touches (for me, that means a lamp with a built-in organizer carousel as its base, with compartments for variously colored pens, markers, pencils, paper clips, a small stapler, and the obligatory *purple* staple-remover). Aesthetics are very important to me, so once I have created a visually appealing writing zone (with some help from my logical left brain), I'm much more likely to enter it—and use it accordingly.

In spite of all this fun with aesthetics and utility, my right brain still feels overwhelmed—as indicated by my endorsement of items 1, 2, 4, and 6. My right brain just can't stand the thought of organizing notes, can't imagine actually having a writing nest that works for me, still prefers to pile rather than file, and is still afraid that even if I am organized, I still won't write. In other words, like most kids, the childlike right side of my brain is great with coming up with ideas, but has difficulty with the follow-through. That's where we all need help from the rest of the brain.

While the right side of the brain can rush easily into the write-or-flight response, both sides of the brain are able to tap into the prefrontal cortex, that front and center section of the brain that provides what neuropsychologists call "executive functioning skills." This is the part of the brain that acts like a well-functioning executive of a company: It knows how to organize and synthesize information, how to plan and carry out activities, and pretty much everything else we need to stay organized enough to get anything done, whether it's writing or doing taxes.

Right now, as you consider the quality of your frontal lobe's executive functioning skills, you might be thinking of that old joke: "Hey, when they were passing out brains, I thought they said *trains,* and I took the last one." Whether or not you grabbed the last godforsaken brain available, for many people, the ability to access executive functioning skills is often eclipsed by the fight-or-flight reaction. Remember, once we go into that write-or-flight reaction it's much more difficult to concentrate—and off we go for that chocolate-doughnuts-and-coffee run (and we don't call it a "run" for nothing). Since chocolate and caffeine both trigger the release of dopamine, a neurotransmitter that helps with energy, focus, and concentration, it's no wonder we don't go scrambling for baked beans or celery sticks.

A Room with a View

I have worked with many clients who actually had well-developed organizational skills, but they just couldn't access them when it came to writing. Others had books on how to organize, but had never read them. So they had never set up their own aesthetically pleasing writing area.

How about you? Can you visualize the ideal writing zone for yourself—one that can be set up now (not the perfect one that you'll have "someday")? Take a moment, close your eyes, and try to visualize what you could create right now, given the parameters of your current living and working areas. Remember: by *visualizing* your writing area, you are giving your sensory-dominant right brain first dibs on all this, and that makes the right brain very happy and, therefore, more cooperative when the time comes to create these changes.

What do you notice? Which colors do you use to make the area appealing to you? Is there a desk, and if so, is it small or large, with or without organizer cubbies in a hutch? What color is the throw rug you'll buy for the area? What kind of organizing system do you visualize—a right-brain piling/cubby hole system, or a left-brain filing/closed cabinets system?

If you're still having trouble, let's clarify where the battle of the brains might be on this one. In this next exercise, circle the number that best represents how you feel about the level of organization you would like to have in your writing area. Answer first with your dominant hand and then with the other hand. Go with your first instinct.

	DOMINANT HAND	
CHAOTIC	0 1 2 3 4 5 6 7 8 9 10	ORGANIZED

	NONDOMINANT HAND	
CHAOTIC	0 1 2 3 4 5 6 7 8 9 10	ORGANIZED

Do your responses startle you, or are they fairly accurate in terms of what you know about your organizational style? Notice which side of the brain rules when it comes to organizing, or not organizing, your writing zone. How much resistance does it get from the other side?

When I responded to this exercise today, I wasn't surprised in terms of the general difference I often see between my two responses to this sort of exercise. However, I was interested to see that my choices were less extreme than I thought they would be. With my dominant hand, I circled an 8, which for me means that I like to be organized, but I'm not rigid about it. At home, in my writing zone, I tend to use a combination of piling and filing, but at work, I try to maintain mostly filing as my M.O.

Similarly, my response with my nondominant hand was to circle a 2, as opposed to the rebellious 0 I'd expected. To me, this indicates that although the right side of my brain doesn't exactly feel like setting up an organizational system, it appreciates the fact that my left brain does. Since the left side of the brain can break tasks into manageable steps, the overwhelmed-at-the-sight-of-clutter right brain is more than happy to step aside—as long as it gets to pick the colors!

Horizontal Organization

Organizing for the Creative Person: Right-Brain Styles for Conquering Clutter, Mastering Time, and Reaching Your Goals, by Dorothy Lehmkuhl and Dolores Lamping, is a great resource that focuses on visual organization—for example, the use of cubbies rather than filing cabinets. The bottom line is this: there is a method to our madness. *Piling is a form of visual organization.* You know exactly where everything is, don't you? Heaven forbid someone else should clean off your desk—you'd never find a thing!

I repeat: Piling is a form of organization. It's simply horizontal, rather than vertical (AKA filing). You know where things are in each of those piles (a character sketch, last month's electric bill, a packet of mints, notes for an essay, and, at the very bottom, last year's taxes). If you wanted to please the left-brained filers of this world, all you'd really have to do is stand your piles upright, put them in a filing cabinet in pocket manila folders, and label the gusseted folders with names like "upper left corner of desk," "center of desk," and "2nd pile from the left"—whatever works for you. That is, of course, assuming you actually want to become a filer.

With all this in mind, let's make some choices in the next exercise (see opposite page). Check off only the items that resonate with your creative self, and feel free to fill in the blanks or change the wording as needed. Be sure to keep in mind that "an organized system and area for writing" can be more right-brained (visual, with cubbies and colors galore), more left-brained (categorical, with one or two filing cabinets), or a combination of these two patterns (perhaps a colorful visual cubby system for active files, along with a filing system for inactive files).

What do you notice as you peruse your responses? How well do the two sides of your brain concur on this issue? Which side of your brain is the one usually in charge? Would you like to alter that in some way?

Perhaps you feel that you "should" or "need to" be organized—but do you really "want" to be organized? Perhaps you can picture your writing area being organized—but forget the rest of the house for now. Can you now say that you "choose" to be organized?

Keep in mind that for the childlike right side of the brain, it's all about aesthetics. Although your right brain may know what it wants—a visually appealing room with a view—it may not exhibit any sense of empowerment about making active choices to reach that goal. Like most children, the right side of the brain can get overwhelmed by the prospect of setting up a writing area and a writing system—with or without colored files, a sky-blue lampshade, and/or a dangling crystal prism to catch and release the light of day.

DOMINANT HAND
I *should* have an organized system/area for writing.
Reason:
I *need to* have an organized system/area for writing.
Reason:
I *want to* have an organized system/area for writing.
Reason:
I *choose to* have an organized system/area for writing.
Reason:
NONDOMINANT HAND
I *should* have an organized system/area for writing.
Reason:
I *need to* have an organized system/area for writing.
Reason:
I *want to* have an organized system/area for writing.
Reason:
I *choose to* have an organized system/area for writing.
Reason:

Just in case the two sides of your brain aren't in agreement about all this, let's do the next exercise (on the following page) to see about cajoling a little cooperation out of them. As usual, respond with your first reactions.

INTERIOR DIALOGUE

DOMINANT HAND:
What stops you from creating an organized area or system for writing?

NONDOMINANT HAND:

DOMINANT HAND:
What would you need in order to get past what's thwarting you?

NONDOMINANT HAND:

DOMINANT HAND:
So how can we go about getting that for you?

NONDOMINANT HAND:

DOMINANT HAND:
Okay, so how about if we _____?

NONDOMINANT HAND:

Again, do you see any responses here that are understandable, given your history and how you respond to structure—or chaos—in general? Were you able to allow the two sides of your brain to work this out?

When I responded to this interior dialogue today, it was quite clear that I'm dealing with a small child who doesn't know the first thing about decorating, but who is willing to trust my more adult side to get things going.

INTERIOR DIALOGUE
DOMINANT HAND: What stops you from creating an organized area or system for writing?
NONDOMINANT HAND: *I can't do it, plus I don't want to*
DOMINANT HAND: What would you need in order to get past what's thwarting you?
NONDOMINANT HAND: *someone else to help me and buy stuff for it?*
DOMINANT HAND: So how can we go about getting that for you?
NONDOMINANT HAND: *I don't even know*
DOMINANT HAND: **Okay, so how about if we** *buy some picture frames and colored file folders and set out a bunch of decorations you can choose from?*
NONDOMINANT HAND: *okay*

Regardless of the way you felt when you first opened this book, let's stop and take stock of where you are now. Are you ready to set up an organizational system for your writing? Are you willing to make a trip to the local office supply shop, or any other store that carries colorful translucent binders, cubbies, baskets, or anything else that might be appealing to you?

Sometimes just looking at these colorful "toys" is enough to get the right brain on your side when it comes to conquering chaos and finding a home for all of those witty, pithy, creative ideas you've jotted down and stuffed in your pockets, wallet, briefcase, glove compartment, or desk drawers for years. Find them a home already! Because home is where the *start* is.

Using RET for "Organized Resistance"

Although this may all sound great on paper (honestly, no pun intended), perhaps we need to move toward giving the logical left side of the brain a bit more power here by challenging some of the beliefs we may not be aware of—beliefs that are wreaking havoc on our ability to get organized for writing.

In working with a writer I'll call Amelia, it soon became apparent to me that her problems with chaos weren't just about writing—it was the way she lived her life. When I asked Amelia how her home was organized during her childhood, she simply laughed. In reality, she had never had a role model for learning how to keep things organized. Her parents had been warm and loving, but neither of them placed much of a priority on house-cleaning. As a result, Amelia didn't either. As I've said so often to clients: *We go for what we know.*

However, Amelia wanted to become more organized. She wasn't particularly interested in using filing cabinets, as her RET chart on the facing page indicates.

A = **Activating Event:**	*My dining room table and my desk are so cluttered that I can't even think about writing until I clear at least one of them off.*

B = **Belief:**	I have no organizational skills.

C = **Consequences:**	I feel agitated and depressed.

D = Dispute (Dispute and disagree with your own beliefs):
But I really want to write. I could divide my dining room table into 6 areas, buy 6 colored plastic bins, and place all the stuff under the table in the same order it is now, and then drape it all with a long, colorful tablecloth. Then I'd have a place to eat, and a place to write. (I'll deal with the plastic bins later, one at a time.)

E = (Effects of changing your own beliefs):
EMOTION: I feel competent and capable.
THOUGHT: I can change the way I organize things, and I don't have to do it all at once. Those colored bins aren't going anywhere, and I won't let all that clutter rule my life anymore.
BEHAVIOR: I'll write for an hour three times a week. I'll ask a friend to come over on 6 separate Saturdays to help me sift through those bins, and then we'll go for coffee.

Once Amelia examined her beliefs, she was able to move forward in creating her writing plan. Now, it's your turn. Remember: Fill in the blanks for A and C. Then go back and try to discern the Beliefs that may be thwarting you. Then address sections D and E.

RATIONAL-EMOTIVE THERAPY

A = ACTIVATING EVENT:

B = BELIEF:

C = CONSEQUENCES:

D = DISPUTE (DISPUTE AND DISAGREE WITH YOUR BELIEFS):

E = (EFFECTS OF CHANGING YOUR BELIEFS):

EMOTION:

THOUGHT:

BEHAVIOR:

As you examine your responses, take note of any changes that occur in your thought process, as well as in your emotional state. Use this approach whenever you feel overwhelmed by chaos.

To Do or Not To Do List

Here is your list for applying what you've learned in this chapter. As usual, check off the items that appeal to you, and add in more actions that you think might help you as well.

	TO DO OR NOT TO DO LIST
	1. Call someone who cares and tell him or her about your organizational style.
	2. Choose your first area to organize—the one that will entice you to write.
	3. Buy supplies (bins, baskets, cubbies) to help you move your piles to create a space for writing.
	4. Buy supplies to help you decorate your new writing zone (tablecloth, placemat, pen/pencil holder—all in your favorite colors).
	5. Stock up on a few cherished snacks or a pizza, and then invite a friend over for a "chaos reduction party," and offer to do the same for him or her.
	6. Decide to read the next chapter of this book.

And of course, give yourself permission to sit down and simply do nothing at your newly organized writing zone. Perhaps you'll start writing by describing what it feels like to see your dining room table again . . .

\#\#\#

CHAPTER 5

Daily or Deadline?

I never put off till tomorrow what I can
possibly do the day after.

OSCAR WILDE

I used to have all kinds of schedules. Years ago,
in the state of Maine, I chose to write my book on
even days and work outside on odd days. When
winter came, I shoveled snow and slept a little
during the day, then stayed up all night to write.

ERSKINE CALDWELL

Writers say two things that strike me as nonsense.
One is that you must follow an absolute schedule
every day. If you're not writing well, why continue
it? I just don't think this grinding away is useful.

EDMUND WHITE

A Daily Dose of Deadlines

"I just about deadlined myself to death." So sayeth Chris, a twenty-six-year-old high school English teacher who yearned to become a novelist, but who also was close to losing his job for not grading his students' papers in a timely manner. Thus, he "never had time to write" because he was always up late into the evening grading papers.

I asked Chris how he had handled his own papers in college. "Well, I got good grades, but at what cost to my health, sanity, and quality of life?" What was more important was cutting it close, gathering too many notes and quotes, and staying up until 4 A.M., dimly aware that, once again, he had somehow "conquered chaos."

Of course, Chris hadn't been aware of all this while he was in college. As we explored the underlying reasons for his procrastination, he mentioned that he'd grown up in a family of heavy gamblers, never knowing when his next meal might come. He soon began to realize that he was born and raised on chaos—so recreating chaos on a daily basis felt familiar to him. In college, waiting until just before a paper's deadline to actually *start writing sentences* was completely normal to him. Fortunately, he didn't procrastinate as much when it came to gathering the information needed to write a paper. However, he would always hope that he'd find just one more quotation or reference that would render his paper absolutely perfect.

And this obsession with perfection had of course carried over into his teaching: he always felt he had to spend an inordinate amount of time grading each paper in order to give as much guidance as possible—to the point that sometimes he would actually rewrite whole sections of a student's paper to illustrate how the student might communicate more clearly. However, as Chris gained insight into the reasons for his penchant for perfectionism and chaotic living, he soon began to release these patterns that had thwarted his life for so many years. For example, once he stopped rewriting his students' papers, he was actually quite surprised to see that he now had time for a social life!

Such perfectionism is only one of many reasons why people procrastinate until they're faced with the wrong end of a deadline. I have worked with many clients who have struggled with perfectionism, which can readily lead to procrastination, because if we don't have enough time to finish something perfectly, we can always say, "Well, if I'd had more time, I could have done better." In other words, we don't ever have to face our limitations. What if we did do the task on time, even early? And what if we still didn't get top honors when it came to being evaluated? Then we'd have to admit we're not so perfect after all.

Such was the case with Malcolm, a talented writer who was held hostage by the gods of perfectionism. He had done well throughout college, but now it was time to graduate—and he could not bring himself to write one final term paper. He only had one last course to complete, and off he'd be—back to the free world at last! But that was part of the problem—so much so that Malcolm didn't turn in the paper, didn't pass the course, and didn't graduate.

Malcolm was so unsure of himself—so convinced that he had to have perfect grades, the perfect line-up of extracurricular activities, and the perfect internship—that he was certain he'd never get a job upon graduation. Although he had a GPA of 3.6, had performed community service, and had excelled during his internship, Malcolm was still convinced he'd never be employed. However, once he discovered this streak of perfectionism that ran through everything he did, Malcolm was finally able to complete that one last term paper, and graduated the following semester.

Where do these expectations of perfectionism come from? Who dumps this garbage in our heads, anyway? We come here as babies, tabula rasa and all that jazz, and somehow go from nonchalantly spitting up on people without a drop of guilt to fearing the negative evaluations of others so much that only perfection will do!

In the case of Edna, a writer in her late fifties, this expectation of perfection had been with her all of her life. Edna was fine when it came to writing, but she couldn't bear the thought of someone else reading her work, even though she yearned to publish her poetry and short stories. She had an entire list of literary magazines and other outlets that published her type of work, but could never decide which poem or story to send to which magazine. Translation: she felt she needed to be sure of the perfect match between any given piece of her writing and the magazine she'd select for sending a query letter. Inevitably, she would fret for so long that she'd miss the submission deadlines once again, and start the process all over again the next month.

However, it soon became apparent that Edna's streak of perfectionism ran a little deeper than she had thought. As we explored her history, Edna admitted that even as a child she felt she had to be perfect in order to please her parents and teachers, especially since her older brother had a medical condition that prevented him from attending school. Somehow, Edna felt that she needed to make up for her brother's disability, to "make the family proud somehow." On the other hand, as she explored some of the bi-vocal exercises used in this book, Edna began to realize that being perfect was also her way of gleaning some attention from her parents, who were understandably caught up in and overwhelmed by the medical demands of Edna's brother.

However, after forgiving herself for being just an ordinary, flawed human being like the rest of us, Edna was on her way to moving forward in her writing endeavors. As she began to come to terms with the idea of sending out "good-enough" poems and stories, Edna was able to target her first literary magazine, and many more thereafter—and finally saw the publication of several of her stories and poems.

There are many other reasons that writers may procrastinate until they've missed the deadline, or perhaps just barely made the deadline. Deadline-driven writing is often adrenaline-driven writing, with the write-or-flight response fueling our energy levels to keep us focused all the way down to the proverbial wire.

You may find yourself adhering to that age-old motto *I work better under pressure.*

I used to feel this way, and when I was younger, this pattern was so familiar that I probably did work better under pressure. When a deadline looms, most of us become anxious, and our adrenal glands are more than happy to blast us with a fire hose of adrenaline. Some people become activated by adrenaline; others are discombobulated by this rush of energy. Since the right brain is the ruler of this fight-or-flight response, that's the side of the brain usually in charge during deadline madness.

But suppose you'd like to become more of a daily writer. How do we go about changing this, if our natural instincts lead us toward deadline-driven writing? I have worked with many writers who can't imagine writing a book or any other writing project by plugging away, day after day. This can be true for academic as well as creative writing. For the academic writing that you may find aversive, you may think, "Why prolong the agony? I'd rather just get it all over with at the end in one sitting." For the creative writing that you may actually want to do, you may think that you absolutely must produce a perfect first draft. So many people think that "having to revise" is a sign of poor writing. However, the reverse is true: It's during the revision process that good writing becomes better writing. Revising is just as important as creating sentences or lines of poetry in the first place! And of course daily or at least frequent (versus deadline-driven) writing is one way to insure that we have enough time to revise.

You have probably read essays by well-established writers who exhort the reader to write every day. For some people, this works.

For others, the concept of daily writing is unfathomable. Whatever your natural rhythms are—and however they were developed—you can decide whether you want to keep them or change them.

Who Says We Have to Write *Every* Day?

As you'll see upon exploring your own patterns in this chapter, we each have a unique capacity to be deadline-driven and/or daily writers. What is most important is that you feel comfortable *choosing* this part of your writing rhythm, whether it's one extreme or the other, or somewhere in between.

Let's examine which side of your brain is tapping away at the computer at 3 A.M. for a 9 A.M. deadline. See what comes up when you respond to this parallel monologue.

DOMINANT HAND
When I think about daily versus deadline-driven writing, I think:
When I think about daily versus deadline-driven writing, I feel:

NONDOMINANT HAND
When I think about daily versus deadline-driven writing, I think:
When I think about daily versus deadline-driven writing, I feel:

Check your answers, and look for patterns. Maybe you're startled by one or more of your responses, or perhaps this is familiar territory for you.

For once, my responses to this parallel monologue actually showed some agreement between the two sides of my brain. They may speak in different voices—my right brain is more emotionally expressive—but the message is the same.

DOMINANT HAND
When I think about daily versus deadline-driven writing, I think:
neither one works for me
When I think about daily versus deadline-driven writing, I feel:
like I'd rather pace myself my way
NONDOMINANT HAND
When I think about daily versus deadline-driven writing, I think:
one is boring; the other makes me mad
When I think about daily versus deadline-driven writing, I feel:
don't tell me what to do!

I suppose it's fair to say that my college days of adrenaline-soaked writing are over, but I'm also not the kind of person who needs to write every day. I know that I'll return to the writing process, even if I take off a week or a month or even a year, because I like to write, and I have some things I'd like to say. The reassurance of a daily pattern of writing isn't something that appeals to me. In fact, it makes me feel pressure, a different kind of pressure from that imposed by a deadline, but pressure nonetheless—like some kind of duty or obligation. And of course the rebellious side of me doesn't want to be told what to do, either.

But the reassurance of a daily writing rhythm may appeal to you. Suppose you've always worked better under pressure, but you'd like to change that. Remember that even though the right side of the brain triggers the adrenaline rush set off by deadline fever, the right brain may actually prefer not to surf those waves of anxiety. The more childlike right side of your brain may crave stability, which might make daily writing much more appealing to you. However, the leap from a deadline to a daily—or even intermittent—writing rhythm may feel impossible for you.

There are many reasons why people can't make this leap. Let's find out more about your motivation in this area. Give your gut instincts the go-ahead as you respond to this checklist, first with your dominant hand and then with your nondominant hand.

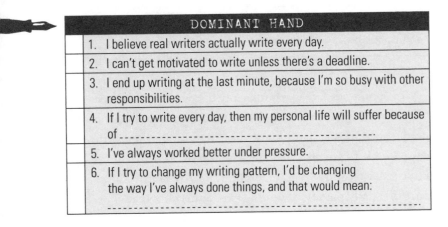

	DOMINANT HAND
1.	I believe real writers actually write every day.
2.	I can't get motivated to write unless there's a deadline.
3.	I end up writing at the last minute, because I'm so busy with other responsibilities.
4.	If I try to write every day, then my personal life will suffer because of _____.
5.	I've always worked better under pressure.
6.	If I try to change my writing pattern, I'd be changing the way I've always done things, and that would mean: _____

	NONDOMINANT HAND
1.	I believe real writers actually write every day.
2.	I can't get motivated to write unless there's a deadline.
3.	I end up writing at the last minute, because I'm so busy with other responsibilities.
4.	If I try to write every day, then my personal life will suffer because of _____.
5.	I've always worked better under pressure.
6.	If I try to change my writing pattern, I'd be changing the way I've always done things, and that would mean: _____.

As you examine your responses, notice any answers that surprise you, as well as the ones that come as no surprise. For example, perhaps you checked off items 3 and 4. You may find that you feel too guilty to write, when you have so much else to do! People are depending on you, and it's hard to say "no" to our loved ones. On the other hand, we get 168 hours every week, and if you only give the world 167 hours, no one's likely to notice. It may be that you decide to write in three twenty-minute blocks each week—whatever you can start with is fine.

At workshops across the country, I've noticed that many writers endorse item number 1 with both hands. In other words, both sides of their brains still cling to the common notion that the only "real" writers are daily writers. I've seen other writers who endorse items 2 and 5—with either or both hands—because they are so locked into their lifelong penchant for working while fueled by adrenaline. One person who endorsed item number 6 with both hands found that part of her felt more relaxed, while another part of her felt that she'd be "a boring adult who always does what she's told." Perhaps you had similar responses, and even though you may know you'd be more relaxed if you gave up your deadline/adrenaline work mode, you still may feel resistant about somehow being controlled by others.

These responses reflect themes of wanting to be in control and of wanting to have more fun and relaxation. The trick, of course, is to work with both sides of your brain whenever you approach the writing process in order to establish a sense of balance between work (writing) and play (relaxation).

The idea of writing frantically on deadline would of course be more appealing to the right side of the brain, which is not only more closely connected to the write-or-flight response, but also tends to see tasks holistically rather than in parts. The idea of parceling out a task into subgoals over the course of several weeks is overwhelming to the childlike right brain. Instead, the right brain puts off the task until it has to be done all at once—the only way the right brain knows how to accomplish anything. It's all-or-nothing in that side of the brain, so we do nothing until the deadline rears its ugly head, and then we do all of the task in one sitting.

On the other hand, we need to remember that deadlines—whether imposed by others or by ourselves—can be helpful. If nothing else, deadlines can drive us to prioritize. If Writing Project B is due before Writing Project A, then we're likely to attack project B first. There may be times when you do feel like you're working under pressure effectively, in which case I'd say, if it isn't broken, don't fix it. However, for other projects, you may find that procrastination prevents you from producing your best work, because you simply don't leave yourself enough time to put forth your best effort. The key here is to allow yourself the luxury of knowing when to write daily, intermittently, and/or at the last minute.

Let's explore these choices in this exercise. On the Likert scale below, circle the number that you find most appealing. Answer first with your dominant hand and then with the other hand.

DOMINANT HAND		
DAILY	0 1 2 3 4 5 6 7 8 9 10	DEADLINE-DRIVEN

NONDOMINANT HAND		
DAILY	0 1 2 3 4 5 6 7 8 9 10	DEADLINE-DRIVEN

Are your responses identical, or radically different, or somewhere in between? Think about which mode you usually choose for completing a writing task, and you'll see which side of your brain is probably in charge most of the time.

I can see that I've found a happy medium in terms of writing intermittently: With my dominant hand, I checked off a well-balanced 4, but with my nondominant hand I checked off an oh-so-surprising 10. (Gee, I wonder which side of my brain steered the ship in college all those years ago.)

Let's make some final calculations regarding your choices about how you feel about daily versus deadline-driven writing. Check off items in this next exercise that resonate for you. For each item, be sure to check the rhythm that feels right: daily, intermittently, or by deadline.

DOMINANT HAND
___ I *should* write: ___ daily ___ intermittently ___ by deadline.
Reason:
___ I *need to* write: ___ daily ___ intermittently ___ by deadline.
Reason:
___ I *want to* write: ___ daily ___ intermittently ___ by deadline.
Reason:
___ I *choose to* write: ___ daily ___ intermittently ___ by deadline.
Reason:

NONDOMINANT HAND
___ I *should* write: ___ daily ___ intermittently ___ by deadline.
Reason:
___ I *need to* write: ___ daily ___ intermittently ___ by deadline.
Reason:
___ I *want to* write: ___ daily ___ intermittently ___ by deadline.
Reason:
___ I *choose to* write: ___ daily ___ intermittently ___ by deadline.
Reason:

Once you know what each side of your brain is telling you, you can choose which of these rhythms works best. Perhaps you prefer one mode, or some combination of the three modes.

When I responded to this exercise, it was clear that part of me still thinks I *should* write daily (the way "real" writers do), even though I've published three books by writing intermittently (which is the way I *want* and *choose* to write)—all the while keeping in mind the fact that I *need* deadlines to help me prioritize.

Here is an interior dialogue to help you nudge the two sides of your brain into working as a team on this one.

INTERIOR DIALOGUE

DOMINANT HAND:
What stops you from effectively managing the time involved in your writing process?

NONDOMINANT HAND:

DOMINANT HAND:
What would you need in order to get past what's thwarting you?

NONDOMINANT HAND:

DOMINANT HAND:
So how can we go about getting that for you?

NONDOMINANT HAND:

DOMINANT HAND:
Okay, so how about if we _____?

NONDOMINANT HAND:

Do your answers reveal any semblance of cooperation between the two sides of your brain? Were you able to reach some conclusions about how to move forward in this area?

When I responded to this interior dialogue today, I noted that my right brain was willing to negotiate—and willing to trust the left side of my brain to take charge of the writing process.

INTERIOR DIALOGUE
DOMINANT HAND:
What stops you from effectively managing the time involved in your writing process?
NONDOMINANT HAND:
I can't decide
DOMINANT HAND:
What would you need in order to get past what's thwarting you?
NONDOMINANT HAND:
help
DOMINANT HAND:
So how can we go about getting that for you?
NONDOMINANT HAND:
you pick it
DOMINANT HAND:
Okay, so how about if we choose together**?**
NONDOMINANT HAND:
okay

Although it may seem odd that I can negotiate this process so readily, keep in mind that I've been listening to both sides of my brain for a long time. Whether this process comes naturally to you or not, you may find that, with repeated exposure to these exercises, the two sides of your brain may meet each other halfway after all. When we can get the two sides of the brain to cooperate with one another, we can more readily adapt or adjust our natural writing rhythms to the demands of daily life.

Let's look at the example of Casey, a retired police officer who wanted to write crime novels. However, he "never seemed to have time," because he was busy volunteering at the local hospital after his wife had died. Here is how a RET chart might look for him.

A = Activating Event:	*I was going to write tonight, but I got called in to volunteer at the hospital.*
B = Belief:	I have to show up—they need me there.
C = Consequences:	I feel relieved, but disappointed in myself. I'll go to the hospital, even though I hate myself for being weak.

D = Dispute (Dispute and disagree with your own beliefs):
I would like to work on that crime novel—it keeps my interest.
I could write for a half hour before I go to the hospital, then maybe write for a half hour in the cafeteria at the end of my four-hour shift.

E = (Effects of changing your own beliefs):
EMOTION: I feel okay about all this—the hospital and the writing.
THOUGHT: Being around people helps me feel better, and writing does, too. I need to do both.
BEHAVIOR: I'll write and go to the hospital tonight.

After Casey was honest with himself, he could see that his beliefs were limiting him—until he actively challenged them, and found a good compromise that worked for him.

Now, it's your turn. Remember: Fill in the blanks for A and C. Then go back and try to discern the Beliefs that may be stopping you. Then work on sections D and E.

RATIONAL-EMOTIVE THERAPY
A = ACTIVATING EVENT:
B = BELIEF:
C = CONSEQUENCES:
D = DISPUTE (DISPUTE AND DISAGREE WITH YOUR BELIEFS):
E = (EFFECTS OF CHANGING YOUR BELIEFS):
EMOTION:
THOUGHT:
BEHAVIOR:

As you examine your responses, notice any changes that occur in terms of your beliefs about yourself and about the writing process. When other situations arise that usually stop you from writing, feel free to use this technique as needed.

To Do or Not To Do List

Below is your list for putting into practice what you've learned in this chapter. As usual, feel free to revise the list according to your needs.

TO DO OR NOT TO DO LIST	
1.	Call someone who cares and tell him or her what you've decided in terms of being a daily, intermittent, or deadline-driven writer.
2.	Write the same thank-you note twice—once with a one-minute timer, and once without a timer. Notice the way you feel about writing when you're under a deadline as opposed to when you're not.
3.	Toast some bread, drop it on the floor, sit down for two minutes, resist the urge to clean it up, and revel in the feeling of being perfectly imperfect.
4.	Decide to read the next chapter of this book.

And above all, allow yourself the luxury of choosing to write daily for a few days, then intermittently for a few days, and catch some deadline-driven writing time while you're at it. It's fine to experiment with all three patterns, depending on your mood and the writing project at hand. What's most important is that you are comfortable with whatever writing rhythm feels best for you on any given day. Flexibility is the key.

# # #

CHAPTER 6

Lunch Hour or Log Cabin?

Writing is like walking in a deserted street.
Out of the dust in the street you make a
mud pie.

JOHN LE CARRÉ

Writing every day is a way of keeping the
engine running, and then something good
may come out of it.

T.S. ELIOT

Temporarily Out of the Office

Like many writers, I used to think that I had to have a huge chunk of time in order to write—whether it was two eight-hour days for a small project, or three months in the mountains tapping away on a manual typewriter in a secluded cabin as far away from so-called civilization as I could get. Without this ideal scenario, I simply couldn't imagine—or attempt—the possibility of writing. So, of course, I didn't write at all.

I've seen this desire for the perfect writing scenario stymie many a writer. I once worked with a brilliant fiction writer who could not bring herself to write unless she left the country for at least two weeks at a time (which her "day job" allowed her to do). She told herself she was gleaning background material for the setting of her novel, but in reality, most of her time was spent chatting and drinking in the local pubs nearest her hotel. Although she craved the solitude offered by this time away from her job at a prestigious magazine, Laura was also uncomfortable with such solitude, and invariably found herself soaking up the local color with a little help from her friends: ale and Irish whiskey.

Although at night she would absorb much about the locale, by day she would usually have forgotten most of the pithy details that would have intensified her novel's setting. Invariably, she would awaken at noon, grab some lunch, sit down to write, and find herself blocked and heading for the nearest tavern by four o'clock. She was dimly aware that she had a drinking problem, and did agree to work on that issue in therapy. However, she had not made the connection between feeling blocked and having too much time on her hands.

Most people have experienced this feeling of being stuck when faced with a large chunk of time, whether the task at hand is writing or cleaning out the garage. This may occur for a variety of reasons, and they are usually emanating from the right side of the brain. Because the right side of the brain sees tasks holistically, rather than in small subtasks, many of us feel overwhelmed when faced with a large task. Similarly, because the right brain sees time holistically, rather than in minutes or hours, it does not deal well with large blocks of unscheduled time, unlike the logical left brain that can divide time for any given task into units of, say twenty or sixty minutes, with breaks in between.

Such was the case with Barbara, an engineer whose left brain could write brilliant software by day, but whose right brain craved that six-month stint in a secluded cabin for completing her novel. Although Barbara had never taken more than one week's vacation per year—though she was entitled to three weeks—she still dreamed of taking a leave of absence from her job. She even knew the place in Vermont where she'd like to stay. However, she always felt guilty about leaving her job, where she truly was indispensable, and her family, where she truly was needed. I asked Barbara if she had ever thought of writing in small chunks of time, say fifteen or twenty minutes, and she looked at me as if I were insane. "I need to be totally away from everyone and everything for a long period of time—I have to be able to concentrate," she replied.

However, I pointed out that she had been able to write her complex software system for her employer in small chunks of time—between phone calls, meetings, and numerous other interruptions. She thought for a moment, then said, "But writing is *different*." She said that she didn't feel she could write her best in a small amount of time—and this was especially problematic for Barbara, because she didn't believe that she should have to revise. I explained to her that writing is somewhat like sculpting: you get the clay, start to shape the face a bit, and then quit for the day—you don't start creating eyelashes before the face is finished!

As we explored this further, it became clear that Barbara could write software in small blocks of time because she felt confident about her skills in that area. However, when it came to writing, she wasn't as confident. So I asked her to try an experiment. I asked her to pick two days during the week when she could write for twenty minutes—about anything related to her novel—during her lunch hour. At first, she hesitated, until I said, "Would you be willing to just try for one day?" She agreed.

The next week, she came back for another session and reported that she had written a scene in the novel—the most potent scene, the turning point, the scene that made her want to write the book in the first place. She was so elated—and so stunned—that she could write so much in such a short amount of time! I pointed out that she had probably been "hyperfocusing," something that we often don't know we can do until we set that egg timer for that allegedly worthless small chunk of writing time. And, perhaps most importantly, although she could see that she had written a good scene, she was actually looking forward to polishing it later. Eventually, Barbara started to write almost every day for twenty minutes, and soon her novel was inching toward completion.

Janus and Sisyphus Strike a Deal

Sometimes when I'm struggling with making time for writing, I can see myself in two different scenes, one as a productive writer, and one as a frantic and blocked writer. At these times, I think about Janus, the Roman god of beginnings. He is usually represented as having two back-to-back heads so he could see in two directions simultaneously. If he were a writer, perhaps he'd have seen two images. The first image might have been one in which he was writing at the times he considered to be most sacred—the first hour of the first day of the first month of the year. Talk about being good with those New Year's Resolutions! In contrast, perhaps with his other head he could only envision himself staring at a blank sheet of slate, his inscribing tool lying motionless in his hand.

In my workshops, I've found that many writers can relate to this comparison. Let's examine how your brain reacts to the notion of time when it comes to writing. Try to respond to the parallel monologue below with your gut instinct, answering first with your dominant hand and then with your nondominant hand.

DOMINANT HAND
When I think about the amount of time I need to write, I think:
When I think about the amount of time I need to write, I feel:

NONDOMINANT HAND
When I think about the amount of time I need to write, I think:
When I think about the amount of time I need to write, I feel:

Notice any surprising answers or trends in your responses to this exercise? Try to think about your answers in terms of what makes you tick (pun intended) as a writer facing the Big Ben of creativity.

My responses to this parallel monologue once again reflect the dichotomy in the philosophies of the two sides of my brain. Here's what Janus had to say today:

DOMINANT HAND
When I think about the amount of time I need to write, I think:
I can write in small chunks of time if I'm up for it
When I think about the amount of time I need to write, I feel:
frustrated sometimes—I can't concentrate

NONDOMINANT HAND
When I think about the amount of time I need to write, I think:
I want a lot!
When I think about the amount of time I need to write, I feel:
mad if I don't get enough time

Yes, once again I am faced with an angry kid who wants it *all now*, and a realistic adult who can see that sometimes I can write in small chunks of time, and sometimes not.

As long as my adult left brain gets some say in the matter, I get some writing done—maybe not an entire screenplay or a grand work of historical fiction, but some writing nonetheless. It just depends on my writing rhythms for that particular day.

For example, earlier today, I felt like Sisyphus with that huge boulder rolling back down on me whenever I tried to climb the hill of creativity. I could barely put a sentence together. So, instead, I typed rote sections of the book, like the blank parallel monologue above, and then pasted them into each chapter for later revision. After lunch, however, my brain clicked on and catapulted right over Sisyphus and the rock and the mountain, and suddenly here I am creating this sentence. As we discussed in Chapter 3, rhythms come and go—and our job as writers is to go with the flow. *Write what you can stand to write at the moment.*

Let's examine the phantom of time in more detail. Check off any items in the next exercise that resonate with you, first with your dominant hand and then with your nondominant hand.

	DOMINANT HAND
	1. I can't write unless I have a big block of time.
	2. I don't believe that writing in small chunks of time will add up to a completed writing project.
	3. If I get a large block of time to write, I end up frittering it away on meaningless or mundane activities.
	4. When I have time to write, I feel guilty about all my other responsibilities (family, relationships, work, chores, etc.).
	5. I never seem to have time to write.
	6. In school and/or in college, whenever I had a large writing project, I would wait for a large block of time before I'd start, and usually I ended up doing it all at the last minute.
	NONDOMINANT HAND
	1. I can't write unless I have a big block of time.
	2. I don't believe that writing in small chunks of time will add up to a completed writing project.
	3. If I get a large block of time to write, I end up frittering it away on meaningless or mundane activities.
	4. When I have time to write, I feel guilty about all my other responsibilities (family, relationships, work, chores, etc.).
	5. I never seem to have time to write.
	6. In school and/or in college, whenever I had a large writing project, I would wait for a large block of time before I'd start, and usually I ended up doing it all at the last minute.

As you peruse your responses, notice any similarities and/or discrepancies between the two sides of your brain. Let's say, for example, that you checked off numbers 1, 2, and 3—with either hand or both hands. Of course the right side of the brain wants instant gratification, and cannot conceive of the possibility of getting something done in small chunks over time. Perhaps you notice that your right brain craves—but can't stand the pressure of—an open eight-hour day for writing. Perhaps you fear that you'd just give in to that feeling of being overwhelmed, and end up frittering away your day at the mall, the grocer's, the dry cleaner's, and Starbucks instead of hanging out with the Muse. If you checked off items 4, 5, or 6 with either hand, you may still be plagued by (1) guilt about taking time out to write, (2) a dearth of time-management skills, and/or (3) a history of waiting for that Big Block of Time that only seems to arrive at 2:00 A.M., the night before the writing project is due.

Let's explore just how much time you really think you need for writing. On the Likert scale below, circle the number that best represents the amount of time you think you need in order to write. Answer first with your dominant hand and then with the other hand. As usual, go with your first instinctive response.

What do you notice? Are the two sides of your brain in sync, or at least close in terms of their estimates?

Mine certainly were not. Today, when I responded to this exercise with my dominant hand, I drew a circle around numbers 3 and 4, which is surprising, since I usually circle either a 5 or a 6—but not both. I suppose I could explain this by noting the fact that I have been writing for quite a while today, and my powers of concentration are of course waning. I need a snack, a snippet of exercise, or both if I am to keep writing. Either way, I feel like my energy is somewhere between a 3 and a 4, so that's all my left brain is asking for at the moment.

DOMINANT HAND												
NO TIME	0	1	2	3	4	5	6	7	8	9	10	MAXIMUM AMOUNT OF TIME

NONDOMINANT HAND												
NO TIME	0	1	2	3	4	5	6	7	8	9	10	MAXIMUM AMOUNT OF TIME

However, with my nondominant hand, I drew a circle around three numbers: 8, 9, and 10! Again, this is unusual for me, since my right brain often demands either a 9 or a 10—but not both. Maybe it's getting fuzzy in my right brain today, since it's obviously cooperating with my left brain *long* enough to write this—and *well* enough to add a dash of creativity to my writing (translation: Janus and Sisyphus were nowhere to be found earlier today).

Let's hone in on your answers to the exercise above. In the following parallel monologue, check off any items that resonate for you, first with your dominant hand and then with your nondominant hand. Be sure to add in the number (0 to 10) that best represents the amount of writing time that fits for each item below, and try to answer the last part of each item in terms of why you've chosen that number.

DOMINANT HAND
I *should* have a chunk of writing time at the level of ... when I write.
Reason:
I *need to* have a chunk of writing time at the level of ... when I write.
Reason:
I *want to* have a chunk of writing time at the level of ... when I write.
Reason:
I *choose to* have a chunk of writing time at the level of ... when I write.
Reason:

NONDOMINANT HAND
I *should* have a chunk of writing time at the level of ... when I write.
Reason:
I *need to* have a chunk of writing time at the level of ... when I write.
Reason:
I *want to* have a chunk of writing time at the level of ... when I write.
Reason:
I *choose to* have a chunk of writing time at the level of ... when I write.
Reason:

Notice how you feel when you respond to these sentences. There's a big difference between "should" and "choose to," isn't there? Your "shoulds" may be unrealistically high or woefully low, depending on whether you want to grab all the time you can for writing, or are feeling guilty about taking time to write at all. Your "needs" and "wants" may reflect a different amount of time that you'd like for writing. But the most important item here is how much writing time you *choose* to have for writing—which may actually be a range of times. In other words, perhaps some days all you can muster up is a 3, while other days you may feel like you can write for hours. When I allow myself my usual range for writing—somewhere between a 2 and an 8 (which for me means a few minutes to a few hours)—then I can accomplish a lot more writing, and have a lot more fun doing it.

The bad news, of course, is that my right brain usually wants a 10, which in right-brain terminology means a solid week with no interruptions. However, the good news is that nowadays my left brain calls the shots on this one, at least most of the time. As you glance at your answers to this exercise, ask yourself which side of the brain tends to be in charge most of the time, as opposed to which side of the brain you would like to be in charge of Big Ben. If you can come to an agreement between the two sides of the brain, or let one side choose what you know can really work for you, fine. If not, use the interior dialogue below to negotiate some kind of settlement.

INTERIOR DIALOGUE
DOMINANT HAND: What stops you from effectively selecting the amount of time you need to write?
NONDOMINANT HAND:
DOMINANT HAND: What would you need in order to get past what's thwarting you?
NONDOMINANT HAND:

INTERIOR DIALOGUE (CONTINUED)
DOMINANT HAND: So how can we go about getting that for you?
NONDOMINANT HAND:
DOMINANT HAND: **Okay, so how about if we** _ _ _ _ _ _ _ _ _ _ _ _ _ _ _ _ _ **?**
NONDOMINANT HAND:

Here's what the two sides of my brain had to say today:

INTERIOR DIALOGUE
DOMINANT HAND: What stops you from effectively selecting the amount of time you need to write?
NONDOMINANT HAND: I'm confused
DOMINANT HAND: What would you need in order to get past what's thwarting you?
NONDOMINANT HAND: courage
DOMINANT HAND: So how can we go about getting that for you?
NONDOMINANT HAND: help me
DOMINANT HAND: **Okay, so how about if we** go with the flow**?**
NONDOMINANT HAND: okay, that's better

Like any child, all my right brain needed was reassurance that someone (that is, my more logical, adult left brain) is in charge, meaning that I can have fun writing—*all in my own good time.*

And you can do the same. Let's add in some RET exercises to solidify your commitment to making active choices about your writing time—regardless of your well-entrenched beliefs about this component of your writing rhythms.

I once worked with a client who was determined to get away for a one-month trip to a secluded location in order to write the first draft of her novel. However, Jessica had been trying to get away for such a trip for ten years—and had never written a word, even though she felt the story was completed in her head. I finally convinced Jessica to settle for taking a two-hour lunch on Tuesdays and Thursdays—a feat that was easily accomplished, given her flexible schedule as an investment banker. However, three weeks into her plan, her car had a flat tire on the way to her local writing café. Here's what her RET chart looked like:

A = Activating Event:	*I have a flat tire, have to get it repaired, can't write today.*
B = Belief:	I have no control over this stupid situation. I won't have time to write until next week!
C = Consequences:	I feel angry and irritated and helpless.

D = Dispute (Dispute and disagree with your own beliefs):
It's only a twenty-minute drive to the auto shop. I do have some handwritten work I could revise while waiting. I guess I can live with only one hour of writing today.

E = (Effects of changing your own beliefs):

EMOTION: I feel better, more at ease.

THOUGHT: I can lower my expectations for this one day. I won't let this car ruin my day.

BEHAVIOR: I'll write for an hour or so while they change the tire. If they change it quickly, I can sit in their lounge and write more before I head back to work.

Although it was difficult for Jessica to lower her expectations again, she allowed herself to be flexible, and took charge of the situation by challenging her beliefs.

Think of a time when your writing time was "stolen away" by some unpredictable factor. See if you can challenge your beliefs, so that if such an unforeseen event occurs again, you'll know how to handle it—and still get some writing done, even if it's the next day. Start with the blanks for A and C. Then go back and identify the Beliefs that may be thwarting you. Then address sections D and E.

Do you notice any shifts in your thinking patterns, and, if so, how do these shifts in thought affect your feelings and behaviors in this potential scenario? Chances are, once you have challenged your beliefs about the situation at hand, you may have a clear view of what needs to be done. Use this approach for other situations that may arise in the future—any time that you need support in your role as a writer.

RATIONAL-EMOTIVE THERAPY

A = ACTIVATING EVENT:

B = BELIEF:

C = CONSEQUENCES:

D = DISPUTE (DISPUTE AND DISAGREE WITH YOUR BELIEFS):

E = (EFFECTS OF CHANGING YOUR BELIEFS):

EMOTION:

THOUGHT:

BEHAVIOR:

To Do or Not To Do List

Here's another list to help you solidify whatever knowledge you may have gleaned from this chapter. And remember: Be sure to remind the right side of your brain that this is really a "to do" *or* a "not to do" list. Choice is the key here.

	TO DO OR NOT TO DO LIST
1.	Call a friend and tell him or her about the chunks of time you'd like to start using for your writing.
2.	Plug these times into your schedule as "sacred" times.
3.	Decide on the minimum amount of time you can start with, for now.
4.	Decide to read the next chapter of this book.

And of course, give yourself permission to write for shorter or longer chunks of time whenever you so choose. The important part is that *you* are choosing.

CHAPTER 7

A.M. or P.M.?

I start working when everyone has gone
to bed. I've had to do that ever since I was
young—I had to wait until the kids were
asleep . . . I've always had to write at night.
But now that I'm established I do it because
I'm alone at night.

JAMES BALDWIN
- - - - - - - - - - - - - - - - - -

When I am working on a book or a story
I write every morning as soon after first light
as possible.

ERNEST HEMINGWAY
- - - - - - - - - - - - - - - - - - - -

I put a piece of paper under my pillow, and
when I could not sleep I wrote in the dark.

HENRY DAVID THOREAU
- -

Having Your Druthers

Just this morning I was thinking, *If I had my druthers . . .* I'd probably write *midday*.

This, for me, was a shock. In the past, I would have filled in the blank with "late at night," as in 10 P.M. until 2 A.M. That was the time, I told myself back then, when I could really concentrate, with no distractions from other people.

Of course, I'd have to start cranking myself up with caffeine about 8:30 P.M., and then keep the IV flowing until about 1:00 A.M. Then, I might wind it down from there—even though I'd want to stay up until 4 A.M., and sometimes did.

But I don't want that now. I know that my best time for writing is from about 10 A.M. until 2:00 P.M., sometimes later in the afternoon, too. But I didn't discover that until I gave up the midnight oil, tried to make myself write dutifully at 8:30 A.M., and found I couldn't do that very well, either.

I've worked with many writers who wanted—or needed—to dump the midnight oil in favor of afternoon tea. I'm reminded of Sheila, a client who realized that burning the midnight oil wasn't cutting it, even though she craved it. She'd end up exhausted the next day, too tired and cranky to enjoy living her life.

When she was in her early twenties, Sheila had thought, *it's just cooler to write late into the night*. Although she didn't realize it at the time, waiting until late in the evening to write was also just one more way for her to avoid the process of writing. Yes, she wanted to write—thought about it on and off all day—but that didn't mean she made writing a priority. Instead, she would do everything else that was on her list for that day (and more), and relegate writing to last place on her list. Sheila had not yet learned how to respect or cherish herself as a writer enough to make writing an integral part of her life.

However, Sheila was now forty-three. She no longer had the physical or mental stamina to be at the height of mental acuity late at night—even with a double mocha java. More importantly, she now had a family of her own, as well as her job as a dental hygienist, so late-night rendezvous with the Muse were no longer possible. It was get up in the morning or else. Although it took some convincing on my part, eventually Sheila allowed her writing patterns to evolve in a number of ways, one of which was learning how to write—effectively—in short blocks of time spaced throughout the day, as opposed to long blocks of time at night.

Many individuals have stopped writing because they couldn't write during their preferred time of day or night. For some people, this was due to family, relationship, or career issues. I worked with one client, Jean, who was a confirmed night-owl writer. However, after having two babies just one year apart, she had not written fiction in over three years, even though she had talent—and the accolades from well-known writers to prove it.

Yet somehow she had managed to squeeze in time to continue her freelance nonfiction writing, "because it generates income."

However, Jean saw fiction in a different light. Like many novelists and writers of short stories, she held this kind of work to more sacred standards—fiction had to be written late at night, for hours at a time. Eventually, she allowed herself to become as pragmatic about writing fiction as she was about writing nonfiction: *Put in the time, and it will get done.* She also joined a writing class, which helped create more incentive for her to finish her novel. Within four months of writing in twenty- to sixty-minute intervals throughout the day (and occasionally at night), she completed her first full draft (albeit for a fully outlined novel she'd started several years earlier).

Right Brain or Bust

Refusing to write because we can't do so at our favorite time of day or night is analogous to a child saying, "If I can't have all the ice cream, I won't have any at all." And that is precisely what the right side of the brain will do, if we allow it. The right side of the brain never grows up, always wants instant gratification, and demands what it wants, whether it's realistic or not. It's rather stubborn, really.

If there's a cardinal rule when dealing with both sides of the brain, it's this: When it comes to the right side of the brain, *don't deny it—supply it. Of course, we may not supply the right side of the brain with exactly what it wants, but instead with something else that may be just as desirable.* For example, writing during the day—in large or small chunks of time—was not appealing to me in the past. My right brain preferred the more romantic, elegant notion of being swathed in the gossamer light of creativity (which of course shows up better if it's dark outside). However, now that I can write during the day—in small or large chunks of time—I find that I look forward to relaxing in the evening. In other words, although my right brain doesn't get to write late at night, I've supplied it with an appealing alternative: reading poetry or fiction.

I have worked with numerous clients who have created a similar adaptation in their writing rhythms, and most of them were quite relieved to let go of the guilt they used to have when faced with the thought of family time, only because these clients hadn't written a word all day. They felt guilty for not writing that day, and guilty for resenting their loved ones who "prevented" them from writing at night. But once these writers harnessed those blocks of writing done during the day—even if only for twenty minutes—they could feel that they had somehow honored their writing selves, and they could then truly enjoy spending time with their loved ones during the evening. The urge to write had been quelled during the day, and no longer plagued them at night. Of course, getting a good night's sleep helped keep these writers alert the next day, so those twenty minute blocks of daytime writing could be even more fruitful.

So, without further ado, let's explore your attitudes about writing at various times of the day. Respond to the items below, first with your dominant hand and then with your nondominant hand.

DOMINANT HAND
When I think about the time of day or night I'd like to write, I think:
When I think about the time of day or night I'd like to write, I feel:

NONDOMINANT HAND
When I think about the time of day or night I'd like to write, I think:
When I think about the time of day or night I'd like to write, I feel:

Look for any similarities or differences among your responses. Are these ideas familiar to you, or have you discovered something new about yourself as a writer? My responses to this exercise reflect pretty much what I already know: I'm better off writing during the day (intermittently, or in blocks of several hours when I get the chance), and I have learned to listen to—but not acquiesce to—my right brain's indecision and guilt about when I choose to write.

DOMINANT HAND
When I think about the time of day or night I'd like to write, I think:
I've chosen my writing times—and daytime is actually better for me
When I think about the time of day or night I'd like to write, I feel:
glad that I'm writing when I'm more alert

NONDOMINANT HAND
When I think about the time of day or night I'd like to write, I think:
I can't decide—it's too hard
When I think about the time of day or night I'd like to write, I feel:
pressured

So that's what my brain had to say about all this. How about yours? Given your reaction to this exercise, you may feel more conflicted than you realized. If, on the other hand, you're not at odds with yourself on this issue, and you like your current time of day or night for writing, then so be it—you're one of the lucky ones! Let's use this next exercise to discern some of the issues that may arise when you try to select a time of day or night for writing. Check off any items that seem accurate for you, and feel free to fill in the blanks accordingly.

DOMINANT HAND
1. I think it's best to write as soon as I wake up, but I rarely do that.
2. I try to write in the evenings, but I'm just too tired.
3. If I write at the time of day I like best, I'd have to give up _____.
4. If I tried to write at my preferred writing time, then _____ might feel _____.
5. When I was in school and/or college, my best time to do writing projects was _____.
6. As a child and/or teenager, when it came time to do written homework, I usually felt: _____.

	NONDOMINANT HAND
1.	I think it's best to write as soon as I wake up, but I rarely do that.
2.	I try to write in the evenings, but I'm just too tired.
3.	If I write at the time of day I like best, I'd have to give up _____.
4.	If I tried to write at my preferred writing time, then _____ might feel _____.
5.	When I was in school and/or college, my best time to do writing projects was _____.
6.	As a child and/or teenager, when it came time to do written homework, I usually felt: _____.

As you peruse your responses, do you notice any trends or perhaps similarities or differences in the way you responded to both lists? Note both of your answers, if any, to numbers 5 and 6. Do you find that the way you handled writing when you were younger is still the same way you handle the writing process? If so, is that the way you'd like to continue to approach written projects?

Perhaps there is a part of you that still hangs on to the notion that writing upon awakening is best—it seems logical to go ahead and do that first—but who says you have to be logical? Maybe you're just not an early-morning person, end of story. Maybe your right brain simply has no interest in writing at 5:00 A.M. (unless, of course, it's at the tail end of an all-night writing binge).

Often, in response to number 4, people will write that *someone else* might feel a certain way if the writer really did use his or her preferred writing time. For example, "my children might feel left out," or "my spouse might feel angry," or "my co-workers might feel slighted if I dodge them at lunch in order to write."

If these issues are pertinent for you, then it may be time to ask yourself, just how much time do you give to the rest of the world? You get 168 hours every week—no more, no less—and what exactly will happen if you take back an hour or two? Timing is important, of course. You don't want to be tapping away on your computer during a family dinner, or when your child's science project is due, or when you've already made a commitment to go to lunch with a colleague.

However, there are moments when you can use small chunks of time wisely, even if it isn't your preferred time for writing. For example, perhaps you find yourself stuck at a garage for several hours while the mechanic repairs your vehicle. You could choose to read the magazines in the lobby, or you could grab a section of your book from your backpack or briefcase and jot away, unperturbed by the fact that it's taking forever to get your car fixed! It's all about being flexible—which side of your brain wants to read magazines and which side wants to write? Maybe doing a little bit of both activities would be a good compromise on any given day.

Think about it: What happens if you tell a 10-year-old to finish up the day's homework prior to dinnertime? Even if that's your household rule, the child may still resist or dawdle, because doing homework isn't usually much fun. However, let's say on this particular day that your child is having great difficulty concentrating. If you give the child a choice, he or she will be more likely to cooperate. For example, you could allow the child to choose between going outside to play with friends for half an hour before dinner or watching a special early TV show before dinner—with the understanding that the child will still complete the homework after dinner. You may not do this every time a child has homework, but sometimes the child may just need a break in his or her routine in order to concentrate.

In much the same way, you can allow yourself the luxury of choice and a sense of control when you select the time(s) of day or night for your writing. Either way, the writing gets done.

Explore your choices in the following exercise. On the Likert scale below, circle the number that you find most appealing. Answer first with your dominant hand and then with the other hand.

DOMINANT HAND												
EARLY IN THE DAY	0	1	2	3	4	5	6	7	8	9	10	LATE AT NIGHT

NONDOMINANT HAND												
EARLY IN THE DAY	0	1	2	3	4	5	6	7	8	9	10	LATE AT NIGHT

Are your responses consistent with earlier choices you've made in these exercises? Or perhaps you have found new discrepancies in your writing preferences. In any event, what's important here is to focus on the time(s) of day or night that feel best to you.

My responses to this parallel monologue are consistent with what I know about my current—versus my past—writing rhythms. With my dominant hand, I circled number 4, but with my other hand, I circled numbers 8 and 9. In other words, my left brain knows that I write best when I start at about 10 A.M., while my right brain still craves those late-night writing binges. I think I circled 8 and 9—as opposed to 10—because even my right brain knows that there are limits to such extremes when it comes to feeling just too tired to write late at night.

Now it's time to make some decisions about your choices in terms of time(s) when you feel most like writing. Check off any items in this next exercise that resonate for you, first with your dominant hand and then with your nondominant hand. For each item, be sure to check the rhythm that feels right: writing during the day or at night.

DOMINANT HAND
I *should* write: ___ during the day ___ at night.
Reason:
I *need to* write: ___ during the day ___ at night.
Reason:
I *want to* write: ___ during the day ___ at night.
Reason:
I *choose to* write: ___ during the day ___ at night.
Reason:

NONDOMINANT HAND		
I *should* write: ___ during the day ___ at night.		
Reason:		
I *need to* write: ___ during the day ___ at night.		
Reason:		
I *want to* write: ___ during the day ___ at night.		
Reason:		
I *choose to* write: ___ during the day ___ at night.		
Reason:		

As you consider the items you selected, notice also the reasons, if any, that you offered, first with your dominant hand and then with your nondominant hand. Notice which side of your brain is actually choosing your current writing times (if any), and whether you prefer this or not. Is it possible that the other side of your brain might have a better feel for what works best for your writing rhythms, given the parameters of your current lifestyle?

In terms of my responses to this exercise, it's clear to me that my left brain is fully aware of my conflicting feelings about writing during the day (I should) and writing late at night (I want to). However, my left brain eventually chooses what's "best for me"—writing during the day. On the other hand, my right brain sounds like a little kid again: I want to write at night so I can "write what I want" and do so "when I feel like it." It's a few minutes after noon as I write this, so you can guess which side of my brain won this battle—at least for today!

If you are still unable to get the two sides of your brain to cooperate in choosing your writing time(s), try the interior dialogue below.

INTERIOR DIALOGUE
DOMINANT HAND: What stops you from choosing the time(s) of day or night you want to write?
NONDOMINANT HAND:
DOMINANT HAND: What would you need in order to get past what's thwarting you?
NONDOMINANT HAND:
DOMINANT HAND: So how can we go about getting that for you?
NONDOMINANT HAND:
DOMINANT HAND: **Okay, so how about if we** _____ **?**
NONDOMINANT HAND:

Does either side of the brain offer any solutions for you? When I responded to this interior dialogue today, I noted that my right brain seems to be lost when it comes to making choices. However, it does seem willing to allow my logical but reassuring left brain to move forward on this one.

INTERIOR DIALOGUE
DOMINANT HAND:
What stops you from choosing the time(s) of day or night you want to write?
NONDOMINANT HAND:
I don't know
DOMINANT HAND:
What would you need in order to get past what's thwarting you?
NONDOMINANT HAND:
the right time
DOMINANT HAND:
Okay, so how about if we *try out some different times and see how it feels***?**
NONDOMINANT HAND:
okay

Clearly, my childlike right brain wants to pick the "right" time. However, perhaps because my right brain knows that my left brain is ready to help, the right side of my brain seems willing to try various writing times—and it's willing to let the left side of my brain make the call on this one (write when you feel like it, if possible).

Let's take a stroll down corpus collosum lane and see how much your "craving" right brain might be willing to allow your "coaching" left brain to make some active choices regarding the time(s) of day—or night—you choose to write.

Craving Versus Coaching

I have worked with many writers who wanted to write in the early morning hours, made plans to do so, and then felt completely thwarted by life just getting in the way. One client, Drake, a single man who worked from 9:00 to 5:00, had finally made the commitment to work on his historical nonfiction book from 6:00 to 7:00 A.M., three days per week. He stated that his brain just "wasn't in writing mode" after a long day at the office. His plan worked well for about a week, and then his hours at worked changed to 8:00 to 4:00. Here is how his RET chart appeared.

A = Activating Event:	*I have to go into work earlier, so now I can't write.*
B = Belief:	I have no control over my supervisor's decision. I'll never get time to write!
C = Consequences:	I feel powerless and angry. I need this job, so I'll just have to give up writing for now.

D = Dispute (Dispute and disagree with your own beliefs):
I can still write—maybe from 5:00 to 6:00 A.M. I'd have to go to bed an hour earlier, but I could tape my favorite television shows and watch them early, the following night.

E = (Effects of changing your own beliefs):
EMOTION: I feel empowered.
THOUGHT: I can revise my schedule, and write and enjoy my shows.
BEHAVIOR: I'll go to bed earlier, tape my shows, and write at 5:00 A.M.

Although it was difficult for Drake to fall asleep earlier, he adjusted his sleep schedule in ten-minute increments over the course of one week. Each night, he'd go to bed another ten minutes earlier than the night before, until his body had adjusted to his new schedule. What was interesting was that Drake got accustomed to being up earlier, and decided to use two mornings a week to work out with weights in his home gym, which he hadn't utilized up to this point. As he put it, "I'll be in shape for my first book-signing!"

Think of a time when some obstacle stopped you from writing at your chosen time of day—or night. Fill in the blanks below, and see if changing your beliefs can help you to change your actions in terms of making time for your writing.

RATIONAL-EMOTIVE THERAPY
A = ACTIVATING EVENT:
B = BELIEF:
C = CONSEQUENCES:
D = DISPUTE (DISPUTE AND DISAGREE WITH YOUR BELIEFS):
E = (EFFECTS OF CHANGING YOUR BELIEFS):
EMOTION:
THOUGHT:
BEHAVIOR:

What do you notice as you peruse your responses? Examine any changes in beliefs, thoughts, and emotions—especially in terms of consequences. Take note of any feelings of empowerment, or at least diminished frustration, as you actively challenge the way you tend to think about your chosen writing time(s). Remember that you can try this exercise whenever you feel stuck—or angry—about not being able to write at the time of day or night that you prefer. Sometimes choosing your second-best writing time is better than no time at all.

To Do or Not To Do List

To help you move forward on the suggestions in this chapter, here is another list for you to act upon—or not—depending on your mood at this very moment.

	TO DO OR NOT TO DO LIST
1.	Call a friend and tell him or her about the time(s) you'll write.
2.	Negotiate one hour of writing time with your loved ones, reminding them you'll still be available the other 167 hours of the week.
3.	Pick the absolute worst time for you to write, set a timer for five minutes, and notice any momentum or excitement elicited by this artificial deadline while you respond to one of the following prompts: 1. As soon as the narrator of my novel entered the mall, he/she headed straight for [name of store], because _____. 2. The first time I ever _____ was incredible, because _____. 3. I was so angry when _____ that I _____ because _____.
4.	Decide to read the next chapter of this book.

And of course, give yourself permission to celebrate the fact that, even with the limitations of your current lifestyle, you can still write at a time of day or night that is reasonably comfortable for you—even if it's your second or third choice—knowing that in the future you may very well be able to write during the time of day or night that ranks as your first choice now.

###

CHAPTER 8

Alone or at Starbucks?

I have to be alone. A bus is good. Or walking the dog. Brushing my teeth is marvelous—it was especially so for *Catch-22.*

JOSEPH HELLER

The solitude of writing is also quite frightening. It's quite close sometimes to madness, one just disappears for a day and loses touch.

NADINE GORDIMER

So the only environment the artist needs is whatever peace, whatever solitude, and whatever pleasure he can get at not too high a cost. All the wrong environment will do is run his blood pressure up; he will spend more time being frustrated or outraged.

WILLIAM FAULKNER

A Matter of Balance

I used to love traveling by plane. I liked the hustle and bustle in the airport, as well as my alone time once I was on the plane. In other words, I craved solitude but needed chaos—a great way to avoid negative feelings that might well up when no other distractions are there to keep it all at bay. Although I didn't realize it for a long time, this was one reason why I loved traveling around the country to conferences, workshops, and seminars, whether I was presenting a problem or not. Now, I choose carefully where and when I'll travel, because the idea of "hiding" from myself in an airport or on a plane is no longer appealing. I'd rather be engaged in my real life, and take time out for writing as I see fit.

I've worked with many clients who could only write under conditions of chaos, as well as with other clients who could write only in total solitude. The fact is, we may need both—that's why it's good to have both a private and a few public places to write. Although after reading Chapter 4 you may have learned how to create your private writing area, you may also need to know when it's time to get out and, armed only with pen and paper (no computers—too distracting), get thee to the nearest diner, restaurant, or café.

For example, I have worked with many clients who craved and also detested the solitude they felt was essential to the writing process. One client, who struggled with ADHD, felt so conflicted that he usually just didn't write at all. On the one hand, Troy felt he needed absolute silence, a distraction-free room, and no interruptions in order to be able to concentrate on his writing. However, no sooner would he achieve this—by locking himself into a library carrel at the university—then he'd feel the itch to talk with someone. The sense of aloneness was unnerving to him, and also downright boring—he needed more stimulation to keep from falling asleep.

What I suggested was for him to modify his writing requirements. In other words, I asked him how he'd feel about writing for twenty-minute blocks of time in the library carrel, and then allowing himself the luxury of text-messaging a friend or checking e-mail for five minutes. In this way, he could hyperfocus on his writing, but the solitude and silence would be time-limited, and therefore perhaps more tolerable and constructive. Troy readily agreed, but knew he'd have to struggle to limit his connection-with-others time to five minutes. He resolved to set a five-minute timer on his watch to jolt him out of his social reverie and to remind him to get back to writing. Because Troy truly enjoyed writing, over time this system eventually worked well for him.

Another client had the opposite problem. Celia found being alone so aversive that she couldn't possibly stand the thought of writing, even though she wanted to write. When I reassured her that absolute solitude was not essential for everyone in order to write, she began to explore some of the reasons she felt so trapped by this paradigm. Celia had grown up in a large family with nine siblings. She had shared a room with five sisters until she moved on to college at age eighteen. Up until that time, she basically had no quiet, private time for herself. No sooner would she start to write a poem or a character sketch than one of her sisters would bounce into the room and try to snatch the paper from Celia's hand—or at best, try to read over Celia's shoulder. As Celia was a very private writer, she felt that she could never write around other people.

On the other hand, Celia was accustomed to being in a bustling household, where someone was always cooking, laughing, watching TV, talking on the phone, or playing card games. Indeed, she had never experienced being truly alone until she went to college and had a roommate who spent most of her time at her boyfriend's apartment. What Celia had to do was find some sort of balance, in which she could feel comfortable with the dim sounds of other people in the background, while at the same time feeling reassured that no one would invade her writing time.

Eventually, Celia found several diners and coffeehouses that were five miles from campus. While she'd write in these relaxing environments, she could hear the familiar tinkling of glasses and silverware, the low hum of conversation and occasional staccato burst of laughter, but she also knew that she wouldn't be interrupted by her friends from the university.

How Much Solitude Is Too Much Solitude?

Perhaps you saw some similarities in the two cases discussed previously in terms of your own writing process. Let's examine your thoughts and feelings about this issue. Try to respond to this parallel monologue with your first reaction to each item, first with your dominant hand and then with your nondominant hand.

DOMINANT HAND
When I think about solitude, I think:
When I think about solitude, I feel:

NONDOMINANT HAND
When I think about solitude, I think:
When I think about solitude, I feel:

As you focus on your answers to this exercise, try asking yourself a few questions. How did you spend time alone as a child—reading, writing, TV, video games? How much outside stimulation did you need to feel comfortable? As a child, were you often home alone after school? Did you feel alone or lonely—or both? The answers to these questions may help you to understand your feelings about the solitude that's sometimes necessary for writing.

My responses to this exercise certainly reflect how I feel now, as well as how I felt when I was younger.

DOMINANT HAND
When I think about solitude, I think:
it's something I can deal with
When I think about solitude, I feel:
okay—but sometimes miss being around others when I'm writing

NONDOMINANT HAND
When I think about solitude, I think:
it's boring unless I have a book to read
When I think about solitude, I feel:
it might be scary or boring

Although my left brain displays a realistic attitude toward solitude, my right brain shows a different side. Feeling scared or bored reflects the diction of a younger voice. The word "bored" is often a catchall phrase for kids who don't want to experience anxiety, anger, or other strong negative emotions. *Boring* means that they are not otherwise occupied, and therefore they might experience negative emotions that would normally be kept at bay by the normal distractions of everyday activities.

Let's examine more closely what lies beneath your attitudes about writing and solitude. As usual, try to respond with your first instincts.

	DOMINANT HAND
1.	I don't usually like solitude.
2.	I need to be alone in order to write.
3.	I never get time alone in order to write.
4.	If I tried to get more alone time to write, then _____ might feel _____
5.	When I was in school and/or college, I usually did my academic work alone.
6.	As a child and/or teenager, when it came time to do homework, I usually felt _____ when other people were around.
	NONDOMINANT HAND
1.	I don't usually like solitude.
2.	I need to be alone in order to write.
3.	I never get time alone in order to write.
4.	If I tried to get more alone time to write, then _____ might feel _____
5.	When I was in school and/or college, I usually did my academic work alone.
6.	As a child and/or teenager, when it came time to do homework, I usually felt _____ when other people were around.

Do you notice any startling responses, or is this fairly familiar turf for you? Do the two sides of your brain display different attitudes about solitude? Perhaps one side of your brain knows it's better to be alone when you're writing, but sometimes you feel better if you are surrounded by others in a local café, where your sensory-dominant right brain can hear the tinkling of ice cubes in glasses, the soft clink of silverware against china, the subtle hum of human voices. Or perhaps your responses to this exercise indicate your awareness that you might feel lonely if you have too much solitude.

Additionally, take note of your responses to the items pertaining to earlier times in your life: are you repeating deeply ingrained patterns of solitude that worked when you were younger, even if these patterns no longer serve you well?

If you're still confused, use this next exercise to explore your options. On the Likert scale below, circle the number that you find most appealing. Answer first with your dominant hand and then with the other hand.

DOMINANT HAND												
NO SOLITUDE	0	1	2	3	4	5	6	7	8	9	10	TOTAL SOLITUDE

NONDOMINANT HAND												
NO SOLITUDE	0	1	2	3	4	5	6	7	8	9	10	TOTAL SOLITUDE

Are your responses fairly predictable, or way out in left field? Notice whether either of your responses correlates closely with what you actually choose in real life. Is there a compromise to be made, or is one side of your brain doing a good job on its own in terms of choosing how comfortable you are with solitude?

When I examine my responses, I can see once again the disparate reactions I display when I access both sides of my brain. With my dominant hand, I circled both numbers 3 and 4, but with my nondominant hand I circled number 10. Although the right side of my brain declares that it *wants to be alone*, my left brain's response is a more accurate reflection of what really happens when I write. Sometimes I do indeed want—and need—to be alone when I write. At other times, I feel edgy with solitude, and seek out a public place to sit with my Muse.

Listening to the muffled sounds of others may be akin to what Dr. Donald Winnicott called being "alone in the presence of the mother." He used this phrase to describe the sense of independence and security that a toddler feels just by having a loving caretaker in the room, even if the child is playing quietly, without interacting with the caretaker. In other words, being "alone in the presence of others" can be soothing. Sometimes just the sight or sounds of other people can be enough to ease our distress about solitude.

Let's clarify your choices about how you feel about solitude and the writing process. Check off any items in this next exercise that resonate for you, first with your dominant hand and then with your nondominant hand. For each item, be sure to check off the rhythm that feels right: being with others, or being alone.

DOMINANT HAND
I *should:* ___ be with others ___ be alone when I write.
Reason:
I *need to:* ___ be with others ___ be alone when I write.
Reason:
I *want to:* ___ be with others ___ be alone when I write.
Reason:
I *choose to:* ___ be with others ___ be alone when I write.
Reason:

NONDOMINANT HAND
I *should:* ___ be with others ___ be alone when I write.
Reason:
I *need to:* ___ be with others ___ be alone when I write.
Reason:
I *want to:* ___ be with others ___ be alone when I write.
Reason:
I *choose to:* ___ be with others ___ be alone when I write.
Reason:

Do your responses reflect what you already knew about your-self, or do they enlighten you with news you hadn't expected? Take a close look at which side of your brain is actively choosing what you want, need, or know is best for you. Is there a need to compromise? If so, what works best for you as a writer—being with others, being alone, or some combination of these two states of being, depending on your mood on any given day?

Let's peer more closely at your preferences in this area. As you respond to the interior dialogue below, remember to go with the first response that pops into your mind.

INTERIOR DIALOGUE
DOMINANT HAND:
What stops you from choosing your level of solitude when you write?
NONDOMINANT HAND:
DOMINANT HAND:
What would you need in order to get past what's thwarting you?
NONDOMINANT HAND:
DOMINANT HAND:
So how can we go about getting that for you?
NONDOMINANT HAND:
DOMINANT HAND:
Okay, so how about if we _____?
NONDOMINANT HAND:

Again, take note of your feelings as you did this exercise. Were the two sides of your brain able to create a solution?

When I responded to this interior dialogue today, I couldn't help but notice how uncertain and powerless the childlike right side of my brain appears. Even though it seems to know what it wants, it has no sense of empowerment in terms of how to achieve the goal of balancing solitude and the writing process. The good news is: my left brain does.

INTERIOR DIALOGUE
DOMINANT HAND: What stops you from choosing your level of solitude when you write?
NONDOMINANT HAND: *I don't know*
DOMINANT HAND: What would you need in order to get past what's thwarting you?
NONDOMINANT HAND: *to decide*
DOMINANT HAND: So how can we go about getting that for you?
NONDOMINANT HAND: *I don't know but I would like a little place just for me!*
DOMINANT HAND: **Okay, so how about if we** *choose together?*
NONDOMINANT HAND: *okay, but not all the same*

It's significant that in this last line, my right brain is casting a small vote for the notion of balancing public and private writing zones. "Not all the same" might be a childlike way of saying both options are viable, and that it's important to be flexible.

The same could be true for you. Let's utilize some RET strategies to help you feel comfortable about whether you choose to write in private, or in a public place.

One client, Eric, decided that he could only write in a public place—he just couldn't imagine writing in total solitude. Eric had chosen a local coffee shop about five miles from his apartment as his writing zone. However, one day, life got in the way. Here is what Eric's RET looked like on that day.

A = Activating Event:	*My car battery is dead, so now I can't write.*
B = Belief:	I can only write at the coffee shop, at my favorite table. I won't be able to write today.
C = Consequences:	I feel sad and powerless. There's no place to write, so I won't. I'll just frantically clean my apartment instead.

D = Dispute (Dispute and disagree with your own beliefs):
I can call a friend to see if he'll drop me off at the coffee shop. I could walk to the library. It's okay for me to try new places for writing.

E = (Effects of changing your own beliefs):
EMOTION: I feel competent in making new choices.
THOUGHT: I can change my writing zone, just for today.
BEHAVIOR: I'll call a friend, or write in the library.

Eric wasn't thrilled about having to write in a different location—he felt "at home" in the coffee shop. However, once he realized that the change needn't be permanent, and that he could choose to get a ride to the coffee shop or walk to the library, he felt more in control. Although he had grown accustomed to writing in public, he also realized that his aversion to being alone stemmed from the loss of a romantic relationship years earlier. As Eric began to finally grieve this loss, he no longer felt afraid to be alone—with his feelings or his writing.

You can also shift your way of thinking. Think of a time when something or someone kept you from writing either in private or in public. Fill in the blanks below, and notice how changing your beliefs may assist you in changing the outcome of this type of situation, so that you can—and will—write anyway.

RATIONAL-EMOTIVE THERAPY
A = ACTIVATING EVENT:
B = BELIEF:
C = CONSEQUENCES:
D = DISPUTE (DISPUTE AND DISAGREE WITH YOUR BELIEFS):
E = (EFFECTS OF CHANGING YOUR BELIEFS):   EMOTION: THOUGHT: BEHAVIOR:

Take a closer look at your answers. Examine any new consequences that may arise once you have challenged—or changed—
your beliefs about the situation in which you feel your writing is
being thwarted.

To Do or Not To Do List

Once again, below you'll find a set of suggestions that you may
use to put into practice what you've learned in this chapter. Pick
only the ones you like, and feel free to add in your own items as
well. After all, it's *your* list.

	TO DO OR NOT TO DO LIST
	1. Call a friend and tell him or her where you plan to write this week.
	2. Ask your friend to meet you at this place after you've had twenty minutes of writing time.
	3. If you would like a private writing zone, spend an hour with a friend setting up the area in the most appealing way for you.
	4. If you would like a public writing zone, spend some time there first, just to get a feel for the place.
	5. Buy yourself a "public writing kit" (portable case or binder with pen holder, favorite type of paper, in favorite colors).
	6. Decide to read the next chapter of this book.

And be sure to give yourself permission to explore both public and private areas for writing. If one doesn't work, you have
plenty of other options—also known as "choices," just in case
your right brain needs a reminder. . . .

CHAPTER 9

Sequential or Non-sequential?

One of the most difficult things is the
first paragraph.

GABRIEL GARCIA MARQUEZ

I always know the ending; that's where I start.

TONI MORRISON

What's so hard about that first sentence is that you're stuck
with it. Everything else is going to flow out of that sentence.

JOAN DIDION

The last thing that we find in making a book is to know
what we must put first.

BLAISE PASCAL

Permission to Skip Ahead

I have worked with many writers who reach a certain point in a writing project—or can't begin the project at all—because they are overwhelmed or stymied by the current section they are addressing. This is especially true for longer projects, such as a doctoral dissertation or a book. However, even when someone is stuck in the middle of a poem or an essay or a short story, I'll offer them "permission" to skip ahead to a section that's easier, and come back to the difficult section later. When they balk at this notion of writing in this flexible manner, I'll ask them if writing sequentially is working right now, and they'll usually say "no." At that point, most writers are usually willing to at least try writing whatever piece of the project they can tolerate.

For example, one client was so overwhelmed by the thirty interviews he'd have to conduct to complete his dissertation that he had never started it, even though the university had approved his proposal two years before. So I asked him what subtask would be the easiest for him to complete. He chose to call the agencies and set up the interviews, and then started to write the introduction to his dissertation. By the time the interviews rolled around a month later, he wasn't so hesitant to conduct them. Having

completed the introductory section to the dissertation by then—
and feeling the mastery that goes with such an accomplishment—
the client felt much more inclined to forge ahead.

In working with another client, Kyle, I found a similar con-
striction of choices. Kyle felt that he absolutely had to write his
novel in sequence, from first to last chapter. I agreed with him
that it might be helpful first to set up his three-act structure:

1. Character needs something/has a problem
2. Situation intensifies
3. Situation gets resolved

However, I had to challenge his notions about perfect chronology when it came to the process of writing his novel.

For over two years, Kyle had been stalled in writing his mystery novel. He had written most of the beginning of the book,
and he knew the ending, but he could not figure out the middle
of the book. What I encouraged him to do was to go ahead and
write the last act of the book. He was astounded at my suggestion,
but agreed to try it.

When he returned the following week, Kyle was happy to
report that he had at last started to write again. He found that by
outlining the end of the book first, he could begin to see some of
the clues he'd have to insert in the middle of the book in order
to make the ending plausible, but not predictable. Eventually, he
began to go back and forth in terms of writing scenes from act
one and act two of the book. Finally, he did finish the manuscript, and began sending it to both agents and publishers.

How Flexible Is Your Muse?

Let's focus on your attitudes about the writing process. See what comes up when you respond to this parallel monologue.

DOMINANT HAND
When I think about sequential versus nonsequential writing, I think:
When I think about sequential versus nonsequential writing, I feel:

NONDOMINANT HAND
When I think about sequential versus nonsequential writing, I think:
When I think about sequential versus nonsequential writing, I feel:

Maybe you're startled by one or more of your answers, or perhaps this is familiar territory for you. My responses to this parallel monologue illustrate the dichotomy that often arises between the two sides of my brain on this issue.

DOMINANT HAND
When I think about sequential versus nonsequential writing, I think:
I like both
When I think about sequential versus nonsequential writing, I feel:
more flexible

NONDOMINANT HAND
When I think about sequential versus nonsequential writing, I think:
it's confusing
When I think about sequential versus nonsequential writing, I feel:
trapped

With my dominant hand, my answers reveal consistency: "I like both" approaches to the writing process, and feel "more flexible" as a result. I know there are times when one approach works better than the other for me.

In contrast, with my nondominant hand, my answers—though consistent with each other—stand in stark contrast to my first two responses. This time, I wrote "confusing," because I don't know what to do when faced with two choices, each of which has its own appeal. Secondly, I wrote that I feel "trapped," for the same reason. Although I was a mischievous child, I was afraid to break the rules blatantly, so it makes sense that the more childlike right side of my brain would feel stuck and unable to make a decision about which type of writing pattern to choose. Of course, there's the implicit assumption here that I'd have to choose between the two; like most children, this part of my brain tends to see choices as "either/or" rather than "and/or." Thank goodness my left brain is more focused on having both spontaneous and sequential approaches to writing!

Let's focus more closely on your attitudes about the writing process. Check off any items that are true for you, and feel free to fill in the blanks as needed.

	DOMINANT HAND
1.	I believe a writing task should be written in chronological order.
2.	If I get stuck in the middle of a project, I feel like I can't move forward on it unless I pick up where I left off.
3.	It's too hard to keep a large writing project in my head all the time, so I end up not writing at all.
4.	If I write sections or chapters for a large writing project out of order, I'll never be able to make sense of it all for the final draft.
5.	If I spontaneously write any section of a writing project that I feel like writing at the moment, then I'd have to give up _____
6.	If I don't write sequentially, I think I would feel _____ because _____
	NONDOMINANT HAND
1.	I believe a writing task should be written in chronological order.
2.	If I get stuck in the middle of a project, I feel like I can't move forward on it unless I pick up where I left off.
3.	It's too hard to keep a large writing project in my head all the time, so I end up not writing at all.
4.	If I write sections or chapters for a large writing project out of order, I'll never be able to make sense of it all for the final draft.
5.	If I spontaneously write any section of a writing project that I feel like writing at the moment, then I'd have to give up _____
6.	If I don't write sequentially, I think I would feel _____ because _____

Do your responses reflect issues you've noted in the past? Try to allow these issues to resonate with your feelings about the writing process. For example, perhaps you fear that if you wrote spontaneously (as opposed to sequentially), you'd have to give up the order that chronology would bring. Or maybe your responses indicate that sometimes you're just too tired to write, and therefore you need to be able to work on whatever part of the writing task you can focus on—or *want* to focus on—at that point.

The Patchwork Quilt Method of Writing

Your "writing-process profile" will not necessarily be the same for every writing task. For example, with a novel, I'm much more likely to start jotting down scenes and ideas before I come up with a rough outline. Then I'll write whatever scene pops into my head during a twenty-minute block of found time, such as a quick trip to a café near my office. Eventually, I'll start placing the scenes into one of three folders (where they may or may not remain): one for Act I (character faces a dilemma), Act II (dilemma is intensified by other factors), and Act III (dilemma is resolved). I use three different colored gusseted file folders, with a backup of three file folders on my computer.

At some point, I'll number the scenes (which are named according to what's relevant for me in that chapter, such as "Church Scene" or "First Scene with Marcie"). When I finally decide to put the scenes in sequential order, I'll *renumber* them accordingly. In other words, the Act I folder would now contain Scenes 1-20; the Act II folder might contain Scenes 21-45; and the Act III folder would hold Scenes 46-60. If you figure about two or three scenes per chapter, this would make for a novel with twenty or thirty small chapters, which is the way I tend to write.

I call this the "patchwork quilt" method of writing: You make the individual patches (scenes) whenever you feel like it, regardless of sequence. Then, you sew the patches together in a lovely pattern. The difference, of course, is that a novel can't be nearly as haphazard as a quilt—but that's fine.

This is simply a nontraditional writing-process profile. Yes, you end up spending more time at the end putting things in order, and that can be confusing. You may even end up writing a scene more than once (take the better of the two, of course). But if you don't have the luxury of being a full-time writer, sometimes eking out a scene here and there may be the best, if not only, approach. Here's how this spontaneous process profile might look, as compared to a more traditional, sequential approach to constructing a novel. Just for the sake of simplicity, let's say the first draft of this novel might take 100 hours.

NONSEQUENTIAL APPROACH TO WRITING
Prewriting: 20 hours
Writing: 40 hours
Editing: 40 hours

SEQUENTIAL APPROACH TO WRITING
Prewriting: 30 hours
Writing: 50 hours
Editing: 20 hours

As you can see, both approaches may end up taking the same amount of time in the long run.

With the first approach (nonsequential), you get the scenes hammered out and then need more time at the end to put them in order—but at least the scenes get written! If you're not feeling particularly eloquent during a small chunk of writing time, you don't have to write the actual scene with dialogue and action. Rather, you can just write a brief description of what the scene will be about. Keep in mind that the first scene of a novel is best begun *in medias res*—in the middle of the story—so why not approach your writing process that way, too? (I call it writing the IMR novel.)

With the second (sequential) approach, you may spend more time prewriting in terms of outlining, perhaps a bit more time with the writing stage (since you may find that ideas don't flow as easily as they would when you let your right brain pick whatever it feels like writing about, regardless of sequence), and a lot less time editing (in terms of placing your scenes in sequential order).

However, you may find that nonfiction requires a reversal. Try starting out with a sequential outline of the chapters, and then write the chapters somewhat spontaneously. In other words, because nonfiction, for most people, is easier to outline, you can try to write the chapters in the order that they'll appear in the book. However, if you feel stuck, switch to another, easier-to-write chapter and come back to the more difficult chapter at another time.

For example, after outlining this book, I kept folders on all twelve chapters, placing ideas and notes in them whenever I'd think of something pertinent. I wrote partial drafts of most of the chapters before I wrote anything at all for the last chapter. However, it's interesting to me that the *first* chapter for which I wrote a **completed** first draft was the *last* chapter! Go figure. I certainly hadn't planned it that way, but one day, Chapter 12 just popped out. In other words, it's possible to be flexible, to build in spontaneity within a sequential writing process (for me, that would be nonfiction), and to build in sequential elements within a spontaneous writing process (for me, that's fiction).

Let's take a closer look at your choices in this next exercise. On the Likert scale below, circle the number that you find most appealing in terms of your writing rhythm. Answer first with your dominant hand and then with the other hand.

DOMINANT HAND												
NONSEQUENTIAL	0	1	2	3	4	5	6	7	8	9	10	SEQUENTIAL

NONDOMINANT HAND												
NONSEQUENTIAL	0	1	2	3	4	5	6	7	8	9	10	SEQUENTIAL

Are your responses relatively predictable? How close are they on the scale? Can you tell which side of your brain is selecting the way in which you write? My responses give a clear indication of who's in charge. I circled numbers 5 and 6 with my dominant hand, indicating that I'm fairly comfortable writing either way, depending on how I feel.

However, with my nondominant hand, I quickly circled number 10—the only way to go for the childlike part of my brain that was taught that the only sensible way to write is sequentially (even though I might rebel against such an edict). Let's see about making some active choices as we examine our underlying attitudes toward the writing process.

DOMINANT HAND
I *should* write: ___ sequentially ___ nonsequentially.
Reason:
I *need to* write: ___ sequentially ___ nonsequentially.
Reason:
I *want to* write: ___ sequentially ___ nonsequentially.
Reason:
I *choose to* write: ___ sequentially ___ nonsequentially.
Reason:

NONDOMINANT HAND
I *should* write: ___ sequentially ___ nonsequentially.
Reason:
I *need to* write: ___ sequentially ___ nonsequentially.
Reason:
I *want to* write: ___ sequentially ___ nonsequentially.
Reason:
I *choose to* write: ___ sequentially ___ nonsequentially.
Reason:

Examine your responses to this exercise. Does one side of the brain appear to be more flexible in terms of the writing process? Perhaps you felt you should write sequentially, but realized that at times you'll be stuck in a spot and may need to jump to another section and gather momentum, then go back to the tough part later. On the other hand, maybe the more childlike part of your brain is still at the mercy of the excellent study skills you learned way back when:

1. Choose a topic.
2. Gather information.
3. Select the main idea.
4. Create an outline.
5. Write some paragraphs.
6. Revise.

I don't think I ever heard a teacher give me permission to use the six steps of writing that I've proposed (see Chapter 3 for fuller descriptions if necessary):

1. Read-writing
2. Co-writing
3. Rote-writing
4. Prewriting
5. Writing
6. Rewriting

For some writing tasks, the first set of instructions work best. But for other writing tasks—particularly large projects like a novel or nonfiction book—the second set of instructions offers a lot more freedom.

Do you feel that you have the freedom to choose between the more traditional writing process and my proposed six-stage process, depending on the task at hand? If you don't know the answer to this question, below is an interior dialogue to help you ascertain just how flexible you can be as you approach this component of your writing rhythm.

INTERIOR DIALOGUE

DOMINANT HAND:
What stops you from deciding whether to write sequentially or nonsequentially?

NONDOMINANT HAND:

DOMINANT HAND:
What would you need in order to get past what's thwarting you?

NONDOMINANT HAND:

DOMINANT HAND:
So how can we go about getting that for you?

NONDOMINANT HAND:

DOMINANT HAND:
Okay, so how about if we _____?

NONDOMINANT HAND:

Were you able to find a solution, at least in part? When I responded to this interior dialogue, my childlike right brain once again needed permission from my trusted adult left brain.

INTERIOR DIALOGUE
DOMINANT HAND: What stops you from deciding whether to write sequentially or nonsequentially?
NONDOMINANT HAND: *I'm not allowed*
DOMINANT HAND: What would you need in order to get past what's thwarting you?
NONDOMINANT HAND: *permission so I don't get in trouble*
DOMINANT HAND: So how can we go about getting that for you?
NONDOMINANT HAND: *you could tell me*
DOMINANT HAND: **Okay, so how about if** *I help us both choose each time we write together?*
NONDOMINANT HAND: *yes, that's good*

As with other exercises in this book, it's clear to me that I need to listen to both sides of my brain when it comes to writing. Because two heads really *are* better than one.

Now, try some more RET to make sure that you allow the left side of the brain to be in charge of the fact that two heads really are better than one. I've worked with many writers who have found this to be especially true when deciding that they needed to leave themselves both options—writing sequentially sometimes, writing spontaneously at other times.

Sometimes, however, a writer may feel that he can only write sequentially. For example, Timothy was working on a nonfiction book that required a substantial amount of research. He could not fathom the idea of writing—or even researching—sections of his book unless he did so chapter by chapter. Additionally, he always wrote at the computer, and did most of his research online. However, on a day on which he had set aside four hours to work on his book, the power went out in his home in the midst of a heavy snowstorm. Timothy panicked. Here's what his RET chart looked like.

A = Activating Event:	*Power went out. Can't use word processor or Google.*
B = Belief:	I can't do any work on my book today.
C = Consequences:	I feel angry and helpless. I can't write Chapter 4, and therefore can't research Chapter 5. I'll just have to wait.

D = Dispute (Dispute and disagree with your own beliefs):
I can revise some of what I've written in Chapters 1 through 3.
I could jot down some ideas for Chapter 7, since I'm pretty clear on what that's about. Maybe I can even write longhand.

E = (Effects of changing your own beliefs):
EMOTION: I feel edgy, but I'm willing to try this.
THOUGHT: I can do this, and correct any mistakes later.
BEHAVIOR: I'll either write Chapter 4 in longhand or brainstorm.

Timothy definitely got a chance to stretch his ready-for-change muscles—that snowstorm lasted for two days! Timothy joked about having to write by the midnight oil, but in reality, he also felt relieved that he had broken free from his rigid way of approaching his book. Although he still preferred to write sequentially and on the computer, in confronting his own belief system Timothy realized that he had other ways to engage in the writing process.

And you can feel the same way. Think of a time when you felt stuck on a writing project—whether at the beginning, middle, or end. How long did you allow your writing process to be stalled? Were you fearful that if you didn't write sequentially, you might break some unwritten rule or leave out something essential to your topic? Try to explore these issues in this next exercise.

RATIONAL-EMOTIVE THERAPY
A = ACTIVATING EVENT:
B = BELIEF:
C = CONSEQUENCES:
D = DISPUTE (DISPUTE AND DISAGREE WITH YOUR BELIEFS):

RATIONAL–EMOTIVE THERAPY (CONTINUED)

E = (EFFECTS OF CHANGING YOUR BELIEFS):

EMOTION:

THOUGHT:

BEHAVIOR:

Peruse your answers. Reflect on any surprises you may have discovered as you responded to this exercise. Use this approach whenever you feel it's necessary to help you break out of a logjam in your writing process.

To Do or Not To Do List

Now that you've traversed the path of this chapter, let's sum up with the list below. As usual, select the items you prefer, and add other options as needed.

	TO DO OR NOT TO DO LIST
	1. Call a friend and tell him or her that you're going to jump into your stalled writing project wherever you darn well please.
	2. Ask your friend to call you back after you've given yourself twenty minutes to work on any part of your writing project, regardless of sequential order.
	3. Go somewhere in public and allow yourself thirty minutes to work on any part of your writing project that strikes your fancy today.
	4. Decide to read the next chapter of this book.

Don't forget to applaud yourself for having the courage to write something out of sequence—especially since you'll probably feel better afterward when you return to the place where you felt "stuck" before. After all, it's *your* work, and you can write it *in medias res* as much as you please. . . .

#

CHAPTER 10

Single Project or Many?

When I feel difficulty coming on, I switch to another book I'm writing. When I get back to the problem, my unconscious has solved it.

ISAAC ASIMOV

In Key West I get up just before daybreak, as a rule. I like being completely alone in the house in the kitchen when I have my coffee and ruminate on what I'm going to work on. I usually have two or three pieces of work going at the same time, and then I decide which to work on that day.

TENNESSEE WILLIAMS

I was never too good a hand at writing for the magazines. I once did a satirical article for *Vogue*, I think it was. On a painter whom I did not admire.

EZRA POUND

Let Me Count the Ways

As writers, we have many avenues for self-expression. Whether you struggle with writing in multiple genres, or try to juggle several projects in the same genre, this chapter is for you.

Just think about it: Ezra Pound writing for *Vogue*? Although many modern-day publishers frown on a writer who dabbles in multiple genres (hence, the need for pseudonyms), there are those who have done so successfully—think of Margaret Atwood (poetry, essays, short stories, novels), Elizabeth Berg (fiction and nonfiction), or Kurt Vonnegut (short stories, plays, novels, essays, college graduation speeches, guest columns for the online Chicago radical rag *In These Times*).

As writers, we need to balance our need for variety and our ability to be flexible. For some writers, being involved in numerous projects is exciting, but for others, the idea of working on more than one writing project at a time can be overwhelming.

For example, one of my clients, David, had a full-time job as a freelance writer for sports magazines, but he yearned for time to work on his fiction. He was also a poet—and a good one, as evidenced by his poetry awards in college. David stated that he felt completely overwhelmed. He needed to write the sports articles to pay his bills, but he wanted to write his fiction and poetry to express his creativity. For many years, he'd had trouble dealing with this dilemma. To top it off, he'd also grown up in a family where the mantra had been, *Stick with one thing and you'll succeed.*

Although he feared being labeled a jack-of-all-trades by his family of origin, David was twenty-eight years old, and decided he could take the wrath of his family if he had to. However, he was not particularly adept at juggling multiple projects, and always felt he had to finish one task before he could start another. I asked David if he'd be willing to try something a little different this time, and he agreed.

He began by experimenting with poetry at 9:00 on Tuesday mornings. He allowed himself an hour, and tried to organize his deadline-driven freelance writing accordingly. At first, he felt terribly guilty, because he was "wasting" an hour of time when he was "not making money." However, he gradually accepted that the fulfillment he got from writing poetry even just one hour a week more than justified taking that hour off from his freelance work. Eventually, he also began to take time—Saturdays from 8:00 to 11:00 A.M.—to "play around" with one of his novels, and decided to keep that as part of his weekly routine. To his surprise, David actually found that he enjoyed his freelance writing much more, once he had satisfied his cravings for creative expression.

On the other hand, I have worked with writers who were trying to juggle way too many writing projects and weren't getting much done at all. Sophia, a mother of three whose husband worked full-time, felt that she had the luxury of staying at home with the children—and with her writing projects. She had several projects simmering at once: a novel, a series of poems, and weekly essays for an online magazine. However, Sophia had underestimated the amount of time she would need to spend with her children, aged 6, 8, and 9. She soon realized that she was barely completing her online essays (for which she received a nominal fee), was doing no other writing, and found herself feeling resentful toward her children.

As we discussed her situation further, it soon became apparent that Sophia held the notion that she should always be doing "more." Her mother had been a workaholic business executive, and Sophia expected that she should be able to accomplish as much as her mother had. Sophia's mother, however, had been good at multitasking, while Sophia was not. Sophia knew she had to make some decisions, for the sake of herself and her children.

We began by exploring a number of alternatives, most of which were unacceptable to Sophia because they made her feel inadequate. Eventually, though, she was able to let go of the need to be like her mother, and decided to change her priorities accordingly. Sophia realized that she wanted to spend more time with her children, just hanging out and playing—without always thinking in the back of her mind, *I should be writing.* When I asked Sophia which of her writing projects was most meaningful to her at this time of her life, she immediately replied, "Poetry."

From there we came up with a plan. Regardless of what she was doing when her children came home from school each day, Sophia decided that she would immediately focus on her kids. They would first have a snack together, talk a bit about the day's events, and do some homework. Then, Sophia would send the children out to play with their neighborhood friends, and she would work on her poetry for a half hour, then start making dinner so the family could eat together when her husband came home.

Sofia found that just knowing she'd have that half hour each day for writing poetry made all the difference to her. She no longer resented the return of her children after school as an intrusion on her writing time, and enjoyed her time with them accordingly. She also stopped writing essays for the online magazine, and put aside her novel for the time being. As a result, she allowed herself to revel in writing poetry, and began submitting her poems to small literary magazines.

Taking Inventory

As is clear from the previous case examples, some of us are better at multitasking than others. Let's take an inventory of your need for variety—as well as flexibility—in terms of the number and type of writing projects you'd like to work on. Answer the questions below, first with your dominant hand and then with your nondominant hand.

DOMINANT HAND
When I think about working on multiple writing tasks, I think:
When I think about working on multiple writing tasks, I feel:

NONDOMINANT HAND
When I think about working on multiple writing tasks, I think:
When I think about working on multiple writing tasks, I feel:

As you search for patterns among your responses, notice how you feel. Do you sense a conflict between what you think versus what you feel about working on multiple projects? In comparing the answers you wrote with your dominant versus your nondominant hand, how are the responses similar or different? My responses to this parallel monologue show both similarities and differences.

DOMINANT HAND
When I think about working on multiple writing tasks, I think:
it's fine if they are different genres
When I think about working on multiple writing tasks, I feel:
overwhelmed
NONDOMINANT HAND
When I think about working on multiple writing tasks, I think:
that's just crazy
When I think about working on multiple writing tasks, I feel:
irritated

I guess multitasking isn't my forte anymore, if I *feel* overwhelmed and irritated by the thought of multiple writing projects. The old gray matter just ain't what it used to be . . .

On the other hand, my responses differ when it comes to how I think about working on multiple projects. My logical left brain feels fine with that, as long as I have the variety of playing with different genres. But my childlike right brain thinks it's just plain crazy to juggle more than one writing project at a time.

You may feel conflicted as well. Let's see if you can gain more clarity when you allow yourself to respond to this next exercise.

DOMINANT HAND
1. I can't balance more than one writing project at a time.
2. I think I should stick to writing in one genre, even though I am interested in writing in two or more genres.
3. If I start another writing project before I finish the first one, then people would think I am _____
4. Because my life is so busy, I can only fit in one writing project at a time.
5. In school and/or college, when it came to juggling several written assignments, I usually felt _____
6. When I was a child and/or teenager, here is what I was told about working on more than one writing project at a time: _____

	NONDOMINANT HAND
1.	I can't balance more than one writing project at a time.
2.	I think I should stick to writing in one genre, even though I am interested in writing in two or more genres.
3.	If I start another writing project before I finish the first one, then people would think I am _____
4.	Because my life is so busy, I can only fit in one writing project at a time.
5.	In school and/or college, when it came to juggling several written assignments, I usually felt _____
6.	When I was a child and/or teenager, here is what I was told about working on more than one writing project at a time: _____

Do you notice anything startling in your responses? If you checked off number 1 or number 4, is it because you really aren't that adept at multitasking, or is it because your time management skills are rusty or nonexistent? If you checked off number 3, is it because you have an inner rule that says *Finish one thing before you start another*? If so, is it time to ditch that rule?

Alternatively, perhaps you checked off number 2 because you are less confident when writing in another genre. If so, perhaps it's time for a brush-up class. If you checked off number 3 or 6, you may find that the way others perceive you has been more important than the way you lead your writing life. Maybe it's intolerable for you to think that others might view you as "scattered." And, finally, if you checked off number 5, perhaps you have a learned association between multiple projects and anxiety.

Let's take a closer look at the bottom-line preferences of the right and left sides of your brain. On the Likert scale below, circle the number that best represents how you feel about working on one (or no) versus many writing projects. Answer first with your dominant hand and then with the other hand. Go with your first instinctive response.

DOMINANT HAND													
NO PROJECTS	0	1	2	3	4	5	6	7	8	9	10		MANY PROJECTS

NONDOMINANT HAND													
NO PROJECTS	0	1	2	3	4	5	6	7	8	9	10		MANY PROJECTS

How closely aligned are the two sides of your brain? Do your answers indicate conflict between the logical left brain and the more emotional (and more easily overwhelmed) right brain? Keep in mind that, compared to the left side of the brain, the right side of the brain is less adept at organizing and conquering chaos.

When I examined my responses to this exercise, I was somewhat surprised. With my dominant hand, I circled both 2 and 3, indicating some ambivalence even from the logical part of my brain that is better at organizing and prioritizing. With my nondominant hand, I actually checked 0—indicating perhaps that my more childlike right brain just does not want to be bothered with all of this hard work! As I recall, the right side of my brain just wants to have fun (with apologies to Cyndi Lauper).

What matters is your ability to make an active choice, regardless of the disagreements between the two sides of your brain. Let's focus on this exercise as a way of exploring your choices. Answer first with your dominant hand and then with your nondominant hand. Be sure to check either "one" or "multiple" projects.

DOMINANT HAND
___ I *should* work on: ___ only one project ___ multiple projects.
Reason:
___ I *need to* work on: ___ only one project ___ multiple projects.
Reason:
___ I *want to* work on: ___ only one project ___ multiple projects.
Reason:
___ I *choose to* work on: ___ only one project ___ multiple projects.
Reason:

NONDOMINANT HAND
___ I *should* work on: ___ only one project ___ multiple projects.
Reason:
___ I *need to* work on: ___ only one project ___ multiple projects.
Reason:
___ I *want to* work on: ___ only one project ___ multiple projects.
Reason:
___ I *choose to* work on: ___ only one project ___ multiple projects.
Reason:

How do you feel about your responses to this exercise? Can you feel the difference between "should" versus "choose to"? Which side of your brain seems to have more say in this matter? Is there part of you that would like to use what I call "the back burner" method of working on more than one writing task at a time? In other words, can you allow some projects to simmer while another one boils? Can you switch them to different burners on your stove of creativity? If you haven't yet managed to do this, try the following interior dialogue. See what comes up when you give both sides of the brain free rein to make active choices.

INTERIOR DIALOGUE
DOMINANT HAND: What stops you from choosing whether to work on only one or more than one writing project at a time?
NONDOMINANT HAND:
DOMINANT HAND: What would you need in order to get past what's thwarting you?
NONDOMINANT HAND:
DOMINANT HAND: So how can we go about getting that for you?
NONDOMINANT HAND:
DOMINANT HAND: Okay, so how about if we _____?
NONDOMINANT HAND:

Do you find any resolution here? Is there a way to negotiate a compromise between the two voices in your brain? I think that I've managed to do so, as illustrated by my responses to this interior dialogue.

INTERIOR DIALOGUE
DOMINANT HAND: What stops you from choosing whether to work on only one or more than one writing project at a time?
NONDOMINANT HAND: *I'm not sure—what if I am wrong?*
DOMINANT HAND: What would you need in order to get past what's thwarting you?
NONDOMINANT HAND: *make a choice*
DOMINANT HAND: So how can we go about getting that for you?
NONDOMINANT HAND: *I don't know. what if I get in trouble?*
DOMINANT HAND: **Okay, so how about if** *I take charge of juggling more than one writing task at a time?*
NONDOMINANT HAND: *okay, especially poems*

As I peruse my responses, it's pretty clear to me that my right brain is afraid of breaking that old rule of "finish one task before you start another." However, it seems to trust that the left side of my brain can handle this.

Regardless of your responses to this exercise, keep in mind that you can make active choices about whether you are going to be a single-project writer or a multiple-project writer. It doesn't matter which one you choose, as long as you—not someone else—is choosing it. And feel free to bounce between the two modes. In other words, let's say you are committed to a single writing project, but you get bored with it. Perhaps by allowing yourself the luxury of playing with another "toy," like any child, your right brain might just go back to that first "toy" with renewed interest.

As I've said before, when it comes to the right brain, *don't defy it, supply it.*

So now that the right side of the brain has been given what it craves, maybe you can allow the left side of the brain to do some serious work in challenging some of your beliefs about the various writing projects you may want to approach.

One of my clients, Brian, was a PhD candidate working on his dissertation, but what he really wanted to do was to write fiction. Here is how his RET chart appeared.

A = Activating Event:	*Chapter 1 of dissertation is due.*
B = Belief:	I don't want to work on it—I'd rather write fiction. If I can't write what I want, then I won't write at all.
C = Consequences:	I feel resentful, frustrated and worthless, because I know I'll miss the deadline for Chapter 1. I'm frozen—I can't write!

D = Dispute (Dispute and disagree with your own beliefs):
It's true that I prefer writing fiction, but I also know I have to write the dissertation to get my degree so I can get a faculty position at a university. I suppose that for every hour that I work on my dissertation, I could set aside a half hour of reward time to use for writing fiction whenever I want.

E = (Effects of changing your own beliefs):
EMOTION: I feel more "balanced" somehow.
THOUGHT: I can do this—I can write both fiction and nonfiction!
BEHAVIOR: I'll set up a timetable for writing Chapter 1, and keep track of the hours I put in, as well as the reward time I can use for fiction-writing later.

As it turns out, Brian did complete Chapter 1 of his dissertation on time. The real challenge was making sure he gave himself the "reward time" he'd earned. During the first week, he didn't give himself his credit for time served in dissertation-land, and his enthusiasm began to wane. However, during the second week, Brian did allow himself some time to write fiction—and to *read* fiction as well. As a result, he reported that he didn't mind working on the dissertation so much after all.

You can find this same kind of relief. Try to imagine a time when your necessary devotion to one writing project made you feel resentful about not having time for a lower-priority but more enjoyable writing project. Did you find yourself blocked—not working on either project? Or did some other issue come up that threw you into confusion about whether to work on just one project or genre, as opposed to more than one project or genre?

See what happens when you respond to these or related issues in this next exercise.

RATIONAL-EMOTIVE THERAPY
A = ACTIVATING EVENT:
B = BELIEF:
C = CONSEQUENCES:
D = DISPUTE (DISPUTE AND DISAGREE WITH YOUR BELIEFS):
E = (EFFECTS OF CHANGING YOUR BELIEFS):
EMOTION:
THOUGHT:
BEHAVIOR:

Are you surprised by your reaction to this exercise? Were you able to change some of your perceptions, and therefore some of your feelings or behaviors? Remember to keep this tool in your back pocket whenever you're in a dilemma about single versus multiple writing projects.

To Do or Not To Do List

The following list can help you to implement what you've learned in this chapter. Take what works for you and ditch the rest. Feel free to add your own items to the list as well.

TO DO OR NOT TO DO LIST
1. Call a friend and tell him or her whether you are going to work on more than one project/genre this week, or whether you prefer to stick to one for now.
2. Select the day and time you'll work on one writing project this week.
3. Select the day and time you'll work on any other writing project this week.
4. Feel free to switch back and forth between projects if you so choose.
5. Decide to read the next chapter of this book.

Of course, give yourself credit for your decision, whether it's to stick to one project or one genre for right now or to expand beyond one project or genre. It doesn't matter so much what you decide this week—you can always change your mind. What does matter, though, is that *you* are the one who makes these decisions—this week and forever after.

\#\#\#

CHAPTER 11

Private
Writer or
Published
Author?

My purpose is to entertain myself first and other people secondly.

JOHN D. MACDONALD

It's much more important to write than to be written about.

GABRIEL GARCIA MARQUEZ

I have long felt that any reviewer who expresses rage and loathing for a novel is preposterous. He or she is like a person who has put on full armor and attacked a hot fudge sundae or a banana split.

KURT VONNEGUT

The Ever-Expanding Universe of Publication

If you are thinking about publishing your work, try to remember that many successful writers before you have struggled with the issues discussed in this chapter. This chapter first focuses upon whether or not you want to publish at all, and then moves on to some of the options in today's publishing market.

This chapter assumes that you are struggling with whether you *want* to publish your work, and if so, in what format. However, if these publishing concerns are currently stopping you from writing, then you need to address that first.

I have worked with writers who felt so confused, conflicted, and intimidated by the thought of publishing that they just stopped writing—and sometimes never started at all. For example, Ralph, a would-be novelist, came to see me upon the advice of a friend, who had told Ralph to *just go ahead and start writing!* However, Ralph was so sure that no one would ever be interested in his book that he had never even started writing the book. He had scenes and lines and plot twists in his head, but he had never dared to put pen to paper. Eventually, when I asked him what the payoff was for not writing, he looked bewildered. Then he thought for a moment, and said, "I don't have to face rejection."

Indeed, Ralph feared not only being rejected by literary critics, but also by his family and friends, all of whom seemed to think he was going to write a blockbuster novel that would propel him into the nearest mansion. He had talked about the book for so long that even he had expectations of spectacular results. However, as we began to discuss the basic plot line of the book, it also became apparent that Ralph was afraid of public exposure. Although the novel was not autobiographical, Ralph feared that others would assume that it was, and he didn't want to be identified as the main character—a neurotic man with a penchant for petty crime.

I asked Ralph to try on a new idea: writing without the intention of publishing. He was initially startled, then smiled. "I never thought of that," he said. However, once he gave himself permission to simply write what he wanted to write, without regard for publication, he began to work on his novel. He agreed not to wander into his "publication anxiety," as I called it, and to stay grounded in the process of writing. He began by selecting three notebooks, one each for jotting down plot ideas, scenes, and lines of dialogue. He stated that he was actually enjoying the process of writing, and that even though he knew someday he would like to publish his work, he would try to keep that separate from the surges in his creativity. Ralph had finally given himself permission to write for himself first—without regard for the opinions of others—and this is what freed him up to fully engage in the writing process once and for all.

Other writers whom I have counseled were more concerned about the autobiographical nature of their work, whether they were writing novels, memoirs, poetry, short stories, or essays. They were of course concerned about the effect of publication on their loved ones, former colleagues, and friends. For example, Linda, an office receptionist who wanted to write a novel based loosely on her life, felt stymied whenever she sat down to write. "What will my mother think?" she'd say over and over again—in part, because she feared her mother's wrath about revealing family secrets, and in part because Linda didn't want her mother to know how sexually active Linda had been as a teenager. She also feared the possibility of lawsuits, knowing that some people in her novel could recognize themselves and retaliate accordingly.

I asked Linda what she knew about the issues involving the publication of autobiographical material. Linda had thought that as long as she changed the names of the actual people she wrote about, she would be safe from charges of libel. She also thought that even if these people did recognize themselves she would still be protected by law since libel is a charge that only applies to false information, and what she was saying was true. However, I had to inform her that she needed to change much more than the names of the characters, so that she wouldn't be sued for invasion of privacy. Under tort law, this means that if someone's private life is damaged by the fact that she is a recognizable character in a publication, then she has the right to sue for invasion of privacy. (This law is harder to apply to public figures, who are presumed to have given up their right to privacy by allowing themselves to be in the public eye.) I advised Linda to seek the advice of an attorney specializing in intellectual property rights in order to find out the most updated information possible.

Linda knew that she had to change the appearance, gender, profession, hometown, and other details of her characters that could lead to the identification of people she had known. She soon learned that it didn't matter if the character with the wandering eye and the need for a punching bag was a surgeon or an attorney—all that mattered, as far as the plot of her novel was concerned, was that this character had a lot to lose professionally if he was exposed for adultery and domestic violence. She began to see that changing her characters, although difficult, became easier to do once she let go of her need to "tell all" to the world about the injustices she had suffered throughout her life. She began to see that relaying her story in a veiled way through the prismed lens of fiction was another way she could not only tell her story, but also a way to help other women trapped in the situation she'd been in for so long.

Other writers have lamented the fact that they are uncomfortable with public exposure. Elaine was focusing on trying to get an agent for her thesis for her MFA in creative writing, which her professor had told her was a publishable novel. Elaine was confident that the professor was right, but procrastinated about seeking out an agent or a publisher, because she couldn't stand the thought of doing book-signings, panel discussions, and radio and TV interviews. She knew it was a long shot that she'd ever have to face these tasks, but just thinking about what she called this "one-in-a-million" possibility made her cringe. She had always detested and feared public speaking. As we began to explore the reasons behind her anxiety about speaking in public, several issues began to emerge.

"First of all, I'm no beauty queen," Elaine said. She was a woman of normal weight and moderate attractiveness, but had always compared herself to her thinner and more attractive sister, who (of course) happened to be a model. As I helped Elaine to see that no one in her audiences would be envisioning her sister beside her, and that the readers in her audiences would be coming to be inspired by what she had to say, not to see what she had to wear, Elaine began to chuckle. She did, however, decide that she would like to upgrade her wardrobe to boost her sense of confidence for public appearances.

However, even after all this progress, Elaine was still stuck. As we explored her feelings further, it soon became clear that Elaine felt that she would have no protection from public intrusion if she were to do even one book-signing. It was as if her audience would be able to see into the deepest recesses of her soul, all the way back to her early childhood. Like many survivors of childhood abuse, Elaine felt that somehow "others will know" without her telling them.

However, as Elaine began to work through that common feeling of being "damaged merchandise," she was able to let go of her shame, and finally realized that her experiences as a child did not define her. She also learned that no matter what question an audience member might ask, she didn't have to answer it. She was allowed to—and needed to—have boundaries, just like everyone else. This awareness in turn freed her up to begin seeking publication for her novel—a goal that she reached by working with a small literary publisher, which, fortunately for her, only required a few public appearances!

To Publish or Not to Publish

In spite of—or perhaps in light of—the issues discussed in these composite case examples, you may decide that you don't want to publish your work, that perhaps your writing really is only for you, or perhaps it is a legacy you'd like to leave behind for your loved ones. You may also feel overwhelmed at the very thought of writing query letters to agents or publishers (see the appendices for tips on this process). Let's take a closer look at how you feel about keeping your writing private, as opposed to making your writing public. Try to respond to this parallel monologue with your first instinctive responses.

DOMINANT HAND
When I think of publishing my work, I think:
When I think of publishing my work, I feel:

NONDOMINANT HAND
When I think of publishing my work, I think:
When I think of publishing my work, I feel:

Notice any similarities or differences between your responses to this exercise. Do your answers make sense to you, or are they a bit perplexing? Which side of your brain has been advising you on the prospect of publication? When I responded to this parallel monologue, I provided answers that reflect some ambivalence about publishing—even though I have already published three books! Here are my responses.

DOMINANT HAND
When I think of publishing my work, I think:
it's a good thing
When I think of publishing my work, I feel:
good

NONDOMINANT HAND
When I think of publishing my work, I think:
maybe someone will get mad
When I think of publishing my work, I feel:
proud but also nervous

Clearly, the logical left side of my brain is quite comfortable with the idea of publishing my work. In contrast, the right side of my brain feels nervous and fears that "someone will get mad." These responses don't surprise me, considering how early in life I learned to placate authority figures. But, as you can see, I'm still writing, in spite of my right brain's reluctance to go public.

Let's examine further some of the reasons why we may feel conflicting emotions about the prospect—and the process—of publication. Check off any items below that seem to resonate with you, and feel free to fill in the blanks as needed.

	DOMINANT HAND
1.	I think that writing for oneself only, with no intention of publication, is a waste of time.
2.	I believe that I should write for myself first, and avoid thinking about an audience.
3.	If I spend time writing, and don't get published, then others might think _____.
4.	If I do get published, then _____ might feel _____
5.	When I think about being published, I don't know how I would handle being in the public eye.
6.	I get completely overwhelmed when I think about writing query letters to agents and editors.
	NONDOMINANT HAND
1.	I think that writing for oneself only, with no intention of publication, is a waste of time.
2.	I believe that I should write for myself first, and avoid thinking about an audience.
3.	If I spend time writing, and don't get published, then others might think _____.
4.	If I do get published, then _____ might feel _____
5.	When I think about being published, I don't know how I would handle being in the public eye.
6.	I get completely overwhelmed when I think about writing query letters to agents and editors.

Examine your answers. Did you check off the same items with both hands? If so, how did you fill in the blanks on those items? Do the two sides of your brain have similar or different reasons to approach—or to avoid—publication? For example, in response to number 3—*what if I don't get published?*—perhaps part of you indicated that others might think you're wasting good time, while another part of you doesn't really care, as long as you have fun while you're writing! Similarly, maybe you have conflicting feelings about getting your work published and about fear of public exposure. Or maybe you're just intimidated by the thought of writing query letters to agents and publishers.

I certainly had some ambivalence when I responded to this exercise today. Although my left brain would feel proud to be published, my right brain would feel nervous if I published my work. Finally, in response to numbers 5 and 6—fear of public exposure—my left brain seems to feel no qualms, but my right brain, in checking these two items, still seems fearful. However, since my logical left brain knows how to establish clear boundaries between me and my audience, and certainly knows how to write effective query letters, I've published books anyway. I suppose you can guess which side of my brain gets to be in charge at book-signings and during media interviews.

On Choosing to Publish—or Not

Keep in mind that, even if you are offered a book contract, you don't necessarily have to sign it. It is always your choice as to how you'll respond to an offer of publication. It is fine to simply say "no," to keep your work just for you or for a few loved ones. On the other hand, it's not always your choice as to whether you'll be offered the opportunity to publish your work. For these and many other reasons, writers often have some degree of ambivalence about publication.

Let's explore how you feel right now about this issue. On the Likert scale below, circle the number that best represents your desired level of public exposure for your written work. Answer first with your dominant hand and then with the other hand.

	DOMINANT HAND	
PRIVATE	0 1 2 3 4 5 6 7 8 9 10	PUBLISHED

	NONDOMINANT HAND	
PRIVATE	0 1 2 3 4 5 6 7 8 9 10	PUBLISHED

Do your responses differ from each other? Can you see which side of your brain may be offering the most resistance—or encouragement—regarding the potential publication of your writing?

My responses to this parallel monologue were as follows: I checked an 8 with my dominant hand, and I checked a 5 with my nondominant hand. I suppose the 8 reflects the fact that I don't want to publish everything I write—some of my writing is just for me, and some of it I reserve for my loved ones. The 5 response did surprise me a bit, until I realized that my more childlike right brain does think it would be pretty cool to be published, but it's also a potentially anxiety-provoking prospect.

Publishing Anxiety

What makes you anxious about publishing? Well, just about any personal issue you might have can be triggered by the specter of a large publishing house looming in the distance. For example, what if you think your writing just isn't good enough? Then perhaps you need to check out books such as *Self-Editing for Fiction Writers: How to Edit Yourself into Print* by Renni Browne and Dave King, or *The Plot Thickens: 8 Ways to Bring Fiction to Life* by the president of Lukeman Literary, Noah Lukeman. What if you fear getting rejection letters? Then perhaps you need to read some of the rejection letters sent out to the likes of John Steinbeck or Charlotte Brontë, courtesy of Andre Bernard's compilation, *Rotten Rejections: A Literary Companion.*

What if you just don't know enough about how to write effective query letters or book proposals (usually required for nonfiction)? Consult books as *Author 101: Bestselling Book Proposals—The Insider's Guide to Selling Your Work* by Rick Frishman and Robyn Freedman Spizman, Noah Lukeman's *The First Five Pages: A Writer's Guide to Staying Out of the Rejection Pile,* or Elizabeth Lyon's *Nonfiction Book Proposals Anybody Can Write: How to Get a Contract and Advance Before Writing Your Book.*

What if you haven't the slightest idea of how to target agents most appropriate for your work? Then you may want to examine literary agent Jeff Herman's annual compilation of information about and interviews with literary agents and editors, *Guide to Book Publishers, Editors, and Literary Agents;* the annually updated

Writer's Market, published by Writer's Digest Books; or the annually updated *Guide to Literary Agents,* also published by Writer's Digest Books. The point is that there is information out there to help you in your journey toward publication.

Another dilemma you may face is whether to self-publish your own work. This is an especially appealing option if you want more creative and financial control over your book. However, even though you will make more money per copy sold, you need to be willing to pay for the up-front costs of publication, actively promote your book, and find a distributor to disseminate your book. With a standard publishing contract, however, all you need to do is the second option: be willing and able to actively promote your book. Either way, your mode of publication is a matter of personal choice, and perhaps it is less important *what* you choose, and more important that *you* are the one making the choice. Additionally, keep in mind that some best-selling books (e.g., *The Celestine Prophecy*) were originally self-published, but through word of mouth began to sell so well that major publishing houses offered to take over the publication process—thereby offering even broader distribution for these books.

Publish or Panic?

Let's create some clarification about your thoughts and feelings regarding the prospect of publishing your work and regarding the prospect of making a conscious decision to remain a private writer. For the items below, check off any sentences that ring true for you, first with your dominant hand and then with your

nondominant hand. Feel free to plug in some reasons at the end
of any items you endorse.

DOMINANT HAND
I *should:* --- keep my writing private --- publish my writing.
Reason:
I *need to:* --- keep my writing private --- publish my writing.
Reason:
I *want to:* --- keep my writing private --- publish my writing.
Reason:
I *choose to:* --- keep my writing private --- publish my writing.
Reason:

NONDOMINANT HAND
I *should:* --- keep my writing private --- publish my writing.
Reason:
I *need to:* --- keep my writing private --- publish my writing.
Reason:
I *want to:* --- keep my writing private --- publish my writing.
Reason:
I *choose to:* --- keep my writing private --- publish my writing.
Reason:

Which of your responses come as a surprise to you? Which
ones do you recognize as old, familiar themes in your life? Regardless of your answers, were you able to actively choose whether or
not you'd like to publish some—or all—of your work?

When I responded to this exercise today, I could see that at least the left side of my brain is consistent—public and private writing are both acceptable to me. However, my right brain is a bit more complicated. Although that side of my brain would say that I "should" and "choose to" keep my writing unpublished, there is also an element of interest—even if it's a scary proposition, it might be fun to publish a book. And it has been!

If your brain is still fighting with itself over all this, try this interior dialogue to see if you can get some resolution.

INTERIOR DIALOGUE
DOMINANT HAND: What stops you from choosing whether to keep your writing private or published?
NONDOMINANT HAND:
DOMINANT HAND: What would you need in order to get past what's thwarting you?
NONDOMINANT HAND:
DOMINANT HAND: So how can we go about getting that for you?
NONDOMINANT HAND:
DOMINANT HAND: **Okay, so how about if we** _____**?**
NONDOMINANT HAND:

Do your answers reflect your present concerns about publishing? In other words, do you still feel nervous about writing query letters or book proposals? If so, keep in mind that your answers may change once you have consulted some resources.

When I responded to this interior dialogue today, I could see that my right brain is still fearful about maintaining privacy and having good boundaries once I have published my work. However, my left brain shows that once again it can take charge and reassure my more childlike right brain that all will be well.

INTERIOR DIALOGUE

DOMINANT HAND:
What stops you from choosing whether to keep your writing private or published?

NONDOMINANT HAND:
I don't know. other people

DOMINANT HAND:
What would you need in order to get past what's thwarting you?

NONDOMINANT HAND:
other people need to get out of my way

DOMINANT HAND:
So how can we go about getting that for you?

NONDOMINANT HAND:
you tell them

DOMINANT HAND:
Okay, so how about if *I'm in charge of setting boundaries?*

NONDOMINANT HAND:
okay

All in all, what really counts here is your ability to work with both sides of your brain in terms of negotiating a reasonable path for your writing career. You may choose to remain a private writer, or you may choose to seek publication. If you do indeed choose the route of publication, keep this in mind: there's a big difference between saying "I got published" and "My book got published." In other words, what's going out on the public stage is your work, not your identity. Look at J.D. Salinger—did his quiet, nonpublic life keep you from reading *Catcher in the Rye*?

Let's see how it goes for you in this last RET exercise. I'll start with Phil, a writer whose work had been published in small literary magazines. As a result, he knew he had talent—but that confidence flew out the window when he received his first rejection letter from an agent. Here's how his RET chart looked.

A = Activating Event:	*Got rejection letter from prestigious agent.*
B = Belief:	I don't have talent. I'll never get published.
C = Consequences:	I feel rejected and stupid.

D = Dispute (Dispute and disagree with your own beliefs):
It's true that this agent declined to represent me, but he did say that he's not taking on new clients. I can target agents who aren't so busy. I have talent; I just have to find the right match.

E = (Effects of changing your own beliefs):
EMOTION: I feel confident again.
THOUGHT: I can do this—someone will like my work.
BEHAVIOR: I'll select five agents and send out query letters.

Phil did send out five more query letters, and after he received five rejection slips—some of which were complimentary of his work—he sent out five more. The agent who opted to represent Phil "absolutely loved" his work, and was able to place it with a reputable publisher in four months. What is one agent's nightmare is another agent's dream come true. The same goes for publishers.

So how about you? Are you ready to face some of the challenges involved with the process of publication? See what happens when you respond to this next exercise.

RATIONAL-EMOTIVE THERAPY

A = ACTIVATING EVENT:

B = BELIEF:

C = CONSEQUENCES:

D = DISPUTE (DISPUTE AND DISAGREE WITH YOUR BELIEFS):

E = (EFFECTS OF CHANGING YOUR BELIEFS):

EMOTION:

THOUGHT:

BEHAVIOR:

Glance through your responses, and see if you can identify the core beliefs that may be stopping you from becoming a published author. And, above all, remember that they are *your* beliefs—so you have the right to change them, anytime.

To Do or Not To Do List

Here's your list of opportunities to put into practice what you've learned from this chapter. Add or subtract items as needed.

TO DO OR NOT TO DO LIST
1. Call a friend and tell him or her whether you are going to send your work out for publication.
2. Learn how to write an effective query letter and/or proposal by reading Noah Lukeman's *The First Five Pages: A Writer's Guide to Staying Out of the Rejection Pile* and/or Elizabeth Lyon's *Nonfiction Book Proposals Anybody Can Write: How to Get a Contract and Advance Before Writing Your Book.*
3. Learn how to revise and improve your writing by reading *Self-Editing for Fiction Writers: How to Edit Yourself into Print* by Renni Browne and Dave King, *The Plot Thickens: 8 Ways to Bring Fiction to Life* by former literary agent Noah Lukeman, and *Author 101: Bestselling Book Proposals—The Insider's Guide to Selling Your Work* by Rick Frishman and Robyn Freedman Spizman.
4. Learn how to target the best agents and publishers *for your type of work* by reading literary agent Jeff Herman's annual compilation of literary agents and editors, *Guide to Book Publishers, Editors, and Literary Agents*; the annually updated *Writer's Market*, published by Writer's Digest Books; or the annually updated *Guide to Literary Agents*, also published by Writer's Digest Books as well as acknowledgements pages of books that are similar in tone or genre to your work (authors often list editors and agents).
5. Decide to read the next chapter of this book.

And by now, I think it's time you give yourself credit for reading nearly all of this book—take time out to celebrate your new life as a writer. Published or not, here you go!

CHAPTER 12

The Writer's Dilemma:

Responsibility Versus Rhythm

When I stop [working], the rest of the day is posthumous. I'm only really alive when I'm working.

TENNESSEE WILLIAMS

Writers . . . live over-strained lives in which far too much humanity is sacrificed to far too little art.

RAYMOND CHANDLER

My eight-year-old son said the other day: "Dad, why don't you write for *fun*?"

ANTHONY BURGESS

Making Your Words Work for *You*

My good friend Abby Nelson once gave me a hand-painted gift: a 4-inch rabbit on a bicycle with a triangular flag that said:

Whimsy Is ≥ Responsibility.

I was so happy when I saw this gift, and I wasn't really sure why. Yes, I got it, but then I "got it" again and again for many years thereafter. I now realize that *rhythm* lies somewhere in between "whimsy" and "responsibility."

But I didn't always know this. I used to think that I had to be writing all the time, and if I wasn't writing, then I was thinking about writing, or feeling guilty about not writing. It took me a long time to learn that writing doesn't have to be an all-consuming passion that wrings the zest out of your life. I gradually learned to exchange this writer's *burden* for a writer's *rhythm*—which implies a syncopated, synchronized, regularly occurring smooth pattern that blends in with the rest of my life's priorities.

However, many writers are plagued by the thought of writing all the time. And it's not necessarily a thought that generates excitement, or even contentment. Instead, it can feel more like the constant weight of what I call Writer's Responsibility (capitalized to give it extra weight, of course, since we often take our role so seriously). No matter what we are doing, we may always feel that we should be writing, so it hangs over us like a huge responsibility or debt that we can never seem to reconcile—always weighing on us, consciously or unconsciously, whether we realize it or not.

This not only takes the joy out of living, but it can also take the joy out of writing. If writing is viewed as a duty, then it can feel like an oppressive weight—your basic literary anvil, if you will—that brings along, uninvited, its nasty little cohort: angst. Of course, we may write in response to angst over our life experiences or the general state of the planet, but if we are feeling *angst about not writing*, the Muse often goes AWOL.

So how do we ditch this oppressive—and obsessive—way of thinking about writing? Well, first we have to decide if we *want* to stop obsessing about writing, because there's always a payoff that comes with Writer's Responsibility.

For instance, in working with Elliot, it became increasingly clear that there were some deep-seated reasons for Elliot feeling stuck in the molasses of Writer's Responsibility. His wife complained that he spent far too much time at his computer trying to write, especially since he didn't usually produce any writing in between bouts of computer solitaire and online pinball. When I asked him how his wife's frustration affected him, Elliott replied, "Well, if she wasn't mad about that, she'd be mad about something else, so I might as well be writing."

As we explored this issue further, however, Elliott began to realize that he had purposely chosen the evening as his time to write, because it allowed him to avoid contact with his wife, whom he saw as a replication of his nagging father. With that payoff in mind, though, Elliott also realized that writing in the evening was the worst possible time for him to choose for expressing his creativity. He was much more of an A.M. writer.

I asked Elliott how he'd feel if he could get along better with his wife and be able to write. Of course, he said he would be delighted, but he hadn't any idea how to go about all this.

I pointed out that when Elliott used "writing time" as a way to avoid his wife, he was engaging in good old-fashioned passive-aggressive behavior. In other words, he was passively expressing his anger toward his wife. Upon my suggestion, Elliott and his wife began seeing a marital therapist, and not long after that Elliott realized that his wife simply wanted to spend time with him. He had been projecting his old feelings of anger toward his father onto his wife, who had no idea that this had been going on. As they began to resolve their issues, Elliott and his wife—who had slipped into her own childhood role as a "needy child"—began to spend more time together during the evening. They also agreed that Elliott should write early in the morning, before the rest of the family was even out of bed. For Elliott, this came as a great relief—his wife was supportive of his writing after all!

I have also worked with writers whose sense of Writer's Responsibility provided a payoff in the realm of fear of intimacy. For instance, Tara, a perennial PhD candidate, had been working on her dissertation for years. As we discussed how she felt about this, Tara agreed that she had received a number of invisible pay-offs by holding herself hostage via Writer's Responsibility. For her, writing—or not writing—was a way to keep herself from being vulnerable in relationships. She couldn't go to this event or to that movie or on that trip—you name it—because she "had" to write.

But then of course she didn't write, for a variety of reasons, one of which was usually some form of regret or longing about depriving herself of the social event she had just declined! Eventually, Tara came to understand that her fear of relationships—which had been compounded by a broken engagement—was keeping her from moving forward, not only in her personal life but in her professional life as well. She stated that she was tired of being known as an ABD (all-but-dissertation) graduate student, and began actively working on becoming a PhD instead.

As I've shared throughout this book, I have also struggled with many of these same issues. There I'd sit, overwhelmed by what psychologists call a double bind: your basic *damned-if-you-do-and-damned-if-you-don't* dilemma. I wanted time to write, which for me really meant time to hide, and then whenever I'd get time to write (read: hide), I'd yearn to be outdoors and/or in the company of others. For me, the responsibility of writing became a way of not really living.

In other words, my intrapersonal issues (issues I carried within myself from past experiences and relationships) kept me from enjoying the benefits of new interpersonal relationships. Essentially, the right side of my brain—ruler of emotions—kept me protected by the notion that, no matter what, *I should be writing*, which of course meant that I didn't write. Instead, I just felt guilty all the time about not really writing. And missed out on a lot of enjoyable experiences with other people.

And yet here I am, years later, writing a book—about writing, no less. I can do this now that I have the courage to listen to the right side of my brain. Of course, my oh-so-logical left brain always knew what to do in terms of writing academic papers. However, my right brain would not allow me to write from my heart. And, now that I'm listening, what has my right brain told me over the years? *Have more fun. Don't work so hard or so much. Take time to experience life, to love and to be loved. And have fun writing, too!* Maybe Saint Augustine was right: "Better to have loved and lost, than never to have loved at all"—to which I might add: "Better to have written *and* lived, than never to have lived at all."

Remember: Your writing rhythm can be integrated into your life. The choice is yours, and yours alone—and *that* is truly the most important writer's responsibility you have. And forget about writing fluff that others may implore you to write. As Kurt Vonnegut once said, "Write the book you were damn well born to write. They'll buy it, or they won't."

Oh, and just in case you were wondering about the meaning of life—why we are here and all that, whether we're writers or not—well, all I can say is *God Bless You, Mr. Vonnegut*, because I think he came up with the best answer of all. In his last book, *A Man Without a Country*, here is what he said:

> *We are dancing animals. How beautiful it is to get*
> *up and go out and do something. We are here on earth*
> *to fart around. Don't let anybody tell you any different.*

###

Author's Note

As was true with my last book *Write*, I am indebted to the experts who have gone before me in creating groundbreaking work that I have adapted for use with the writing process. Although a thorough discussion of the contributions offered by these theorists, clinicians, and researchers is beyond the scope of this book, the reference list in this book offers further reading.

I am indebted to experts in the area of brain research, such as Dr. Allan Schore *(Affect Regulation and the Repair of the Self)*, Dr. R. Joseph *(The Right Brain and the Unconscious)*, Dr. Fredric Schiffer *(Of Two Minds: The Revolutionary Science of Dual-Brain Psychology)*, and Dr. James Iaccino *(Left Brain-Right Brain Differences: Inquiries, Evidence, and New Approaches)*. These experts and many others have provided anecdotal and empirical evidence about the inner workings of—and differences between—the brain's left hemisphere (logical, language-based, more "adult") and the brain's right hemisphere (emotional, sensory-based, more childlike).

As you explore the exercises in this book, you may—or may not—note differences in your responses, depending on which side of your brain is "answering" the question. However, you may also note similarities and/or "reversals" between the general domains ruled by each side of the brain. This may be due to individual differences, as well as to early childhood experiences, which can affect brain development. For example, chronic and/or acute stressors during early childhood can engender changes in brain development that may cause reversals in areas of hemispheric dominance, less "cooperation" between the two sides of the brain, and/or a higher potential for activating the fight-or-flight response—which I often refer to as the write-or-flight response.

Additionally, I am thankful for the work of researchers such as Dr. James Pennebaker *(Writing to Heal)* and Drs. Stephen Lepore and Joshua Smyth (*The Writing Cure),* who have provided solid empirical evidence that writing, particularly about stressful experiences, can improve health and emotional well-being. As a result of the work published by these researchers—as well as clinicians who adapted techniques from Gestalt psychotherapy, such as Dr. Lucia Capacchione *(The Power of Your Other Hand: A Course in Channeling the Inner Wisdom of the Right Brain)* and John Bradshaw (*Homecoming)*—I was able to develop an approach for breaking through the logjam of procrastination and creative blockage. I call it the bi-vocal approach, because it involves listening to the "voices" of both the left and right sides of the brain in order to cajole these two hemispheres into cooperating—not competing—when it comes to creative work and task completion. Additionally, as an extra boost for the empowerment of the more logical left side of the brain, I have included some cognitive-behavioral exercises drawn from Dr. Albert Ellis's Rational-Emotive Therapy. *However, please note that the bi-vocal approach is not intended as a substitute for psychotherapy. If mental health services are needed, the services of a competent mental health professional should be sought.*

In other words, two heads may actually be better than one. I used both sides of my brain to write this book—and here it is in your hands. I'm glad you came along for the ride.

Appendix A:
Your Write Type

The summary sheet on the following page is for you to jot down your preferences regarding the ten components of a writer's "type." Simply circle the numbers that best represent how you feel about each aspect of your life as a writer. After filling this out, tape it next to your computer, or some other place where you can remind yourself every day who you are—and how you are—as a writer!

MY WRITING PROFILE

	0	1	2	3	4	5	6	7	8	9	10	
NO COMMITMENT	0	1	2	3	4	5	6	7	8	9	10	FULL COMMITMENT
ASLEEP	0	1	2	3	4	5	6	7	8	9	10	HYPER-ENERGIZED
CHAOTIC	0	1	2	3	4	5	6	7	8	9	10	ORGANIZED
DAILY	0	1	2	3	4	5	6	7	8	9	10	DEADLINE-DRIVEN
NO TIME	0	1	2	3	4	5	6	7	8	9	10	MAXIMUM AMT. OF TIME
EARLY IN THE DAY	0	1	2	3	4	5	6	7	8	9	10	LATE AT NIGHT
NO SOLITUDE	0	1	2	3	4	5	6	7	8	9	10	TOTAL SOLITUDE
NONSEQUENTIAL	0	1	2	3	4	5	6	7	8	9	10	SEQUENTIAL
NO PROJECTS	0	1	2	3	4	5	6	7	8	9	10	MANY PROJECTS
PRIVATE	0	1	2	3	4	5	6	7	8	9	10	PUBLISHED

One week/month later . . . How many times have we tried to follow a certain plan, only to find that it doesn't work—and so we just give up? Well, since I don't want that to happen, below you'll find an exact replica of the chart you just filled out. This second version is for any revisions you might choose to make in describing your writing profile. It's O.K. to revamp your strategy!

MY WRITING PROFILE

	0	1	2	3	4	5	6	7	8	9	10	
NO COMMITMENT	0	1	2	3	4	5	6	7	8	9	10	FULL COMMITMENT
ASLEEP	0	1	2	3	4	5	6	7	8	9	10	HYPER-ENERGIZED
CHAOTIC	0	1	2	3	4	5	6	7	8	9	10	ORGANIZED
DAILY	0	1	2	3	4	5	6	7	8	9	10	DEADLINE-DRIVEN
NO TIME	0	1	2	3	4	5	6	7	8	9	10	MAXIMUM AMT. OF TIME
EARLY IN THE DAY	0	1	2	3	4	5	6	7	8	9	10	LATE AT NIGHT
NO SOLITUDE	0	1	2	3	4	5	6	7	8	9	10	TOTAL SOLITUDE
NONSEQUENTIAL	0	1	2	3	4	5	6	7	8	9	10	SEQUENTIAL
NO PROJECTS	0	1	2	3	4	5	6	7	8	9	10	MANY PROJECTS
PRIVATE	0	1	2	3	4	5	6	7	8	9	10	PUBLISHED

Appendix B:
Prevailing over the Perils of Publication

Selecting an Agent or Publisher

Just how do you know if an agent or a publisher is the one for you? The resources listed below can offer more information, but let's just get a few things straight to help you deal with the process of seeking out an agent or editor.

Agents and editors are not a homogeneous group: They all have their likes and dislikes, preferences and pet peeves.

Therefore, it's helpful to do a bit of research on them before you send a query letter. You can do this by checking their Web sites and by consulting the books listed below. Find out whether they publish only fiction or nonfiction, and what types of books they are interested in representing or publishing (mystery, spiritual, women's issues, psychology, travel, children's books, etc.).

You can also target agents and editors who might be interested in your type of book by perusing the acknowledgements pages in books that are similar in topic, tone, style, or format to your book. Authors usually thank their agents and editors on this page. If not, you can contact the publisher and ask who the editor and/or agent was for the author on this particular book.

Be sure to: Write concise query letters. DO NOT send an entire manuscript. If an agent or editor responds to your query letter, be sure to send him *exactly* what he or she has requested: "outline and first fifty pages" or "proposal and two sample chapters" or "entire manuscript")—*no more, no less.*

Remember: You are seeking someone who will be a good fit for you, and agents and editors are always looking for fresh ideas.

Writing a Query Letter

For most people, writing a query letter is a daunting task: How do we explain our books in just a few sentences, and make them sound interesting and unique?

The resources listed below can help with the details, but let's just master a few concepts here to make query letters seem like nothing more than what they are: simple letters asking if someone is interested in previewing our books for representation (agent) or publication (editor).

- Less is more! No more than half a page!
- Key elements to include:
  - Title of your book
  - The "hook" of your book (what makes it unique or different from similar books)
  - Brief sentence or two about the book's contents
  - Sentence about why you are an expert or a person uniquely qualified to write and promote this book
  - Sentence about the intended audience, and the fact that this book may sell as well as a previously published bestselling book *[insert name of book here]* on the same topic, in the same tone, or perhaps of the same format

Remember: It's just a simple letter. Short, sweet, and simple.

Writing a Book Proposal

Writing a book proposal is intimidating for most people, but it doesn't have to be. There's a formula, with a number of variations depending on whose approach you follow, but book proposals all have a certain number of very basic elements in common.

If your book is nonfiction, agents and editors often want to see the proposal before you finish writing the book, in case they want to help shape or slant the book a certain way to reach a broader market. (If your book is fiction, proposals are less often requested; usually the agent or editor will want to know that the novel is completed before you query them, and then they'll want a brief synopsis and the first few chapters.) A book proposal usually has six sections, and is sent along with two sample chapters.

Basic Elements of a Book Proposal

Overview: Contains the "hook" of the book—and gives brief description of contents.

Competition: Describes other books that show an established market for this type of book, but you then state how your book is different (the hook) or improves upon the ideas used in previously published similar books.

Market: Describes the market for your book: who will buy this book? (General public is best, but you may add in "bulk sales for corporations," "libraries," "college students," or any other special groups that may especially want your book.)

Promotion: Details what you'll do to help promote the book—book tours, media appearances, writing articles for magazines, workshops, etc.

About the Author: Provides information about you that establishes you as the best person or expert to write this particular book.

Table of Contents: A list of the book's front matter (such as acknowledgements page, dedication page, list of illustrations), chapter titles, and back matter (appendix, bibliography, index).

Remember: A book proposal should only be as long as it needs to be—ten, fifteen, twenty pages—plus have a few sample chapters attached.

Learning from Rejection Slips

If this isn't the hardest part of the publication process, I don't know what is. No matter how resilient we are, it still feels awful when someone "rejects" our work. However, here are key points that may help you to rebound from rejection letters, and maybe even learn from them.

- Agents and editors have varying tastes in terms of books they'd like to publish.
- Publishing houses have a certain number of titles they publish each year.
- Publishing houses may not accept your book because they've just published one on your topic—though they may not always tell you this.
- Resist the urge to call an agent or editor—it tells them you're not savvy about the publishing industry. (Agents and editors, who are interested primarily in making book sales, pretty much just call each other during the day. They

are not going to use up their precious 9 to 5 hours by talking to us. They read our query letters and book proposals in the evenings and on weekends. Put yourself in their shoes, and you'll find you have more patience in waiting for a written response to your query letters.)

- There are different types of rejection letters:
  - **Boilerplate** ("This isn't right for our book list"). Boilerplate with a few comments from an agent or editor (often sound advice, such as intensifying a novel's plot line, or adding a section to a nonfiction book, or taking a book in another direction).
  - **Written letter/e-mail from an agent/editor** (good, because they've taken the time to write to you personally and to make suggestions about your work; sometimes they'll ask you to resubmit your book with the revisions they've requested).

Remember: It only takes one agent or editor to publish your work; your job is to remain diligent and fearless in sending out queries until you find someone who will want to publish your work.

The Writer's Nemeses: Prevailing over the Perils of Personal Relationships

It's easy to write in a vacuum, not so easy to write in the world of relationships. Here are two examples that illustrate the use of assertiveness (in increasing levels of escalation) for speaking with others who may be thwarting your writing.

As usual, *be aware of any negative consequences that may result from your assertiveness*—for example, getting fired from a job. Sometimes, it's just better to keep quiet and find another way to handle your writing without speaking directly to the person who is thwarting you. You may also want to tailor the intensity of your assertiveness, depending on the type of personal—or impersonal—relationship you have with the other person, as in the two examples below.

First and Foremost: Your non-verbal behaviors are essential to effective communication.

- *Eye contact:* direct (not glaring or wavering)
- *Tone of voice:* calm and sincere (*not* angry/loud or apologetic/whiny/giggly)
- *Attitude:* maintain respect (avoid sarcasm or derogatory comments)

FOUR TYPES OF ASSERTIVENESS (IN ORDER OF ESCALATION)		
Being assertive with an academic advisor:		
Simple Assertion	Initial contact	I'd like to make an appointment to talk about my dissertation.
Empathic Assertion	Professor doesn't respond to your e-mail.	I know you're very busy, but I'd like to set up a twenty-minute appointment to talk about my dissertation.
Confrontive Assertion	Professor didn't show up for meeting.	I know we agreed to meet yesterday for a twenty-minute appointment, but perhaps there was a miscommunication. Let's reschedule.

FOUR TYPES OF ASSERTIVENESS (IN ORDER OF ESCALATION)		
Being assertive with an academic advisor:		
Angry Assertion	Professor has missed several meetings with you	I've tried to meet with you several times about my dissertation, but things haven't worked out, and I know you're very busy. I think it would be best for me to select another advisor.
Being assertive within a personal relationship:		
Simple Assertion	Initial contact	I'd like to use this hour for my writing.
Empathic Assertion	Loved one doesn't respond, or responds negatively.	I know you're tired, but I'd like you to take the kids out for ice cream while I write for an hour.
Confrontive Assertion	Loved one doesn't respond, or responds negatively.	I know we agreed that I would write for an hour on Tuesday evenings, so I'd like you to respect our agreement.
Angry Assertion	Loved one doesn't respond, or responds negatively.	I feel angry that you're backing out on our agreement, and I want you to honor what you've promised me.

Remember: We all have the right to be treated with respect, even when we make mistakes. It's all about revision, *n'est-ce pas?*

Balch, James F., and Phyllis A. Balch. *Prescription for Nutritional Healing: A Practical A-to-Z Reference to Drug-Free Remedies Using Vitamins, Minerals, Herbs & Food Supplements, 3rd edition* (Garden City Park, NY: Avery Publishing Group, 2000).

Berg, Astrid. "The Management of Traumatic Stress Disorder in Infants." *Journal of Child and Adolescent Mental Health* 18, no. 1 (June 2006): pp. 23–25.

Bernard, Andre. *Rotten Rejections: A Literary Companion* (Wainscott, NY: Pushcart Press, 1990).

Bradshaw, John. *Homecoming: Reclaiming and Championing Your Inner Child* (New York: Bantam, 1990).

Bremner, J.D., et al. "Magnetic Resonance Imaging–Based Measurement of Hippocampal Volume in Posttraumatic Stress Disorder Related to Childhood Physical and Sexual Abuse—A Preliminary Report." *Biological Psychiatry* 41, no. 1 (1997): pp. 23–32.

Brewin, Chris R., and Hayley Lennard. "Effects of Mode of Writing on Emotional Narratives." *Journal of Traumatic Stress* 12, no. 2 (April 1999): pp. 355–361.

Browne, Renni, and Dave King. *Self-Editing for Fiction Writers: How to Edit Yourself into Print, 2nd edition* (New York: HarperCollins, 2004).

Capacchione, Lucia. *The Power of Your Other Hand: A Course in Channeling the Inner Wisdom of the Right Brain* (Portland: Borgo Press, 1988).

Charlton, James, ed. *The Writer's Quotation Book: A Literary Companion* (Wainscott, NY: Pushcart Press, 1991).

De Bellis, Michael D., et al. "Brain Structures in Pediatric Maltreatment-Related Posttraumatic Stress Disorder: A Sociodemographically Matched Study." *Biological Psychiatry* 52, no. 11 (November 2002): pp. 1066–1078.

Ellis, Albert, and Robert A. Harper. *A New Guide to Rational Living* (No. Hollywood, CA: Wilshire Book Company, 1975).

Esar, Evan, ed. *The Dictionary of Humorous Quotations* (New York: Bramhall House, 1989).

Ferrari, Joseph R., Judith L. Johnson, and William G. McCown. *Procrastination and Task Avoidance: Theory, Research, and Treatment* (New York: Plenum Press, 1995).

Frishman, Rick and Robyn Freedman Spizman. *Author 101: Bestselling Book Proposals—The Insider's Guide to Selling Your Work* (Avon, MA: Adams Media, 2005).

Gil, Eliana. *Outgrowing the Pain: A Book for and about Adults Abused as Children* (New York: Dell, 1988).

Goring, Rosemary, ed. *Larousse Dictionary of Writers* (New York: Larousse Kingfisher Chambers, 1994).

Heim, Christine, Gunther Meinlschmidt, and Charles B. Nemeroff. "Neurobiology of Early-Life Stress." *Psychiatric Annals* 33, no. 1 (January 2000): pp. 18–26.

Henderson, Bill, and Andre Bernard, eds. *Pushcart's Complete Rotten Reviews & Rejections* (New York: Pushcart Press, 1998).

Herman, Jeff. *Guide to Book Publishers, Editors, and Literary Agents 2007.* (Stockbridge, MA: Three Dog Press, 2006).

Iaccino, James F. *Left Brain-Right Brain Differences: Inquiries, Evidence, and New Approaches* (Hillsdale, NJ: Lawrence Erlbaum Associates, 1993).

Joseph, R. *The Right Brain and the Unconscious: Discovering the Stranger Within* (New York: Plenum Press, 1992).

Karl, Anke, et al. "A Meta-analysis of Structural Brain Abnormalities in PTSD." *Neuroscience & Biobehavioral Reviews* 30, no. 7 (July 2006): pp. 1004–1031.

King, Stephen. *On Writing* (New York: Pocket Books, 2002).

Kitterle, Frederick L., ed. *Hemispheric Communication: Mechanisms and Models* (Hillsdale, NJ: Lawrence Erlbaum Associates, 1995).

Klauser, Henriette Anne. *Writing on Both Sides of the Brain: Breakthrough Techniques for People Who Write* (New York: HarperSanFrancisco, 1987).

Lamott, Anne. *Bird by Bird: Some Instructions on Writing and Life* (New York: Pantheon Books, 1994).

Lehmkuhl, Dorothy, and Dolores Cotter Lamping. *Organizing for the Creative Person: Right-Brain Styles for Conquering Clutter, Mastering Time, and Reaching Your Goals* (New York: Three Rivers Press, 1993).

Lepore, Stephen, and Joshua Smyth. *The Writing Cure: How Expressive Writing Promotes Health and Emotional Well-Being* (Washington, DC: American Psychological Association, 2002).

Lindfors, Petra, and Ulf Lundberg. "Is Low Cortisol Release an Indicator of Positive Health?" *Stress and Health: Journal of the International Society for the Investigation of Stress* 18, no. 4 (October 2002): pp. 153–160.

Lukeman, Noah. *The First Five Pages: A Writer's Guide to Staying Out of the Rejection Pile* (New York: Fireside, 2000).

Lukeman, Noah. *The Plot Thickens: 8 Ways to Bring Fiction to Life* (New York: St. Martin's Press, 2002).

Lundberg, U., and M. Frankenhauser. "Pituitary-Adrenal and Sympathetic-Adrenal Correlates of Distress and Effort." *Journal of Psychosomatic Research* 24 (1980): pp. 125–130.

Lyon, Elizabeth. *Nonfiction Book Proposals Anybody Can Write: How to Get a Contract and Advance Before Writing Your Book.* Rev. ed. (New York: Perigee, 2002).

Mate, Gabor. *Scattered: How Attention Deficit Disorder Originates and What You Can Do about It* (New York: Plume, 1999).

Mayell, Mark. *Natural Energy: A Consumer's Guide to Legal, Mind-Altering, and Mood-Brightening Herbs and Supplements* (New York: Three Rivers Press, 1998).

McEwen, Bruce S. "The Neurobiology and Neuroendocrinology of Stress: Implications for Posttraumatic Stress Disorder from a Basic Science Perspective." *Psychiatric Clinics of North America* 25, no. 2 (June 2002): pp. 469–494.

McFarlane, Alexander C., Rachel Yehuda, and C. Richard Clark. "Biologic Models of Traumatic Memories and Posttraumatic Stress Disorder: The Role of Neural Networks." *Psychiatric Clinics of North America* 25, no. 2 (June 2002): pp. 253–270.

Moore, B. "Cortisol, Stress, and Depression." *British Journal of Psychiatry* 181, no. 4 (October 2002): p. 348.

Murphy, Kevin R. *Out of the Fog: Treatment Options and Coping Strategies for Adult Attention Deficit Disorder* (New York: Hyperion, 1995).

Parkes, Colin, Joan Stevenson-Hinde, and Peter Marris, eds. *Attachment Across the Life Cycle* (New York: Routledge, 1991).

Passons, William R. *Gestalt Approaches in Counseling* (New York: Holt, Rinehart & Winston, 1975).

Pennebaker, James. *Opening Up: The Healing Power of Confiding in Others* (New York: Avon Books, 1991).

Pennebaker, James. *Writing to Heal: A Guided Journal for Recovering from Trauma and Emotional Upheaval* (Oakland, CA: New Harbinger Publications, 2004).

Peterson, Karen E. *The Tomorrow Trap: Unlocking the Secrets of the Procrastination-Protection Syndrome* (Deerfield Beach, FL: Health Communications, 1996).

Peterson, Karen E. *Write: 10 Days to Overcome Writer's Block. Period.* (Avon, MA: Adams Media, 2006).

Plimpton, George, ed. *The Writer's Chapbook: A Compendium of Fact, Opinion, Wit, and Advice from the Twentieth Century's Preeminent Writers* (New York: Viking, 1989).

Schiffer, Fredric. *Of Two Minds: The Revolutionary Science of Dual-Brain Psychology* (New York: Free Press, 1998).

Schore, Allan N. *Affect Dysregulation and Disorders of the Self* (New York: W.W. Norton, 2003).

Schore, Allan N. *Affect Regulation and the Origin of the Self: The Neurobiology of Emotional Development* (Hillsdale, NJ: Lawrence Erlbaum Associates, 1994).

Schore, Allan N. *Affect Regulation and the Repair of the Self* (New York: W.W. Norton, 2003).

Schouwenburg, Henri C., et al., eds. *Counseling the Procrastinator in Academic Settings* (Washington, DC: American Psychological Association, 2004).

Schwartz, Jeffrey M. *Brain Lock: Free Yourself from Obsessive-Compulsive Behavior* (New York: ReganBooks/HarperCollins, 1996).

Shapiro, Francine, and Margot Forrest. *EMDR: The Breakthrough Therapy for Overcoming Anxiety, Stress, and Trauma* (New York: Basic Books, 1998).

Starkman, Monica N., et al. "Improvement in Learning Associated with Increase in Hippocampal Formation Volume." *Biological Psychiatry* 53, no. 3 (February 2003): pp. 233–238.

Storr, Anthony. *Solitude: A Return to the Self* (New York: Free Press, 1988).

Teicher, Martin H., Susan L. Andersen, Ann Polcari, Carl M. Anderson, et al. "Developmental Neurobiology of Childhood Stress and Trauma." *Psychiatric Clinics of North America* 25, no. 2 (June 2002): pp. 397–426.

Thayer, Robert. *Calm Energy: How People Regulate Mood with Food and Exercise* (New York: Oxford University Press, 2001).

Thayer, Robert. *The Origin of Everyday Moods: Managing Energy, Tension, and Stress* (New York: Oxford University Press, 1997).

Vermetten, Eric, and J. Douglas Bremner. "Circuits and Systems in Stress: II. Applications to Neurobiology and Treatment in Posttraumatic Stress Disorder." *Depression and Anxiety* 16, no. 1 (January 2002): pp. 14–38.

van der Kolk, Bessell. "Integrating Basic Neuroscience and Clinical Realities: A Comprehensive Treatment Approach to Complex Post-Traumatic Stress Disorders." Paper presented at conference on Psychological Trauma: Maturational Processes and Therapeutic Interventions, Boston University School of Medicine, Division of Psychiatry, March 10–11, 2000, Boston, MA.

van der Kolk, Bessell, O. van der Hart, and C. Marmar. "Dissociation and Information Processing in Posttraumatic Stress Disorder," *Traumatic Stress* (New York: The Guilford Press, 1996).

Villarreal, Gerardo, et al. "Reduced Hippocampal Volume and Total White Matter Volume in Posttraumatic Stress Disorder." *Biological Psychiatry* 52, no. 2 (July 2002): pp. 119–125.

Villarreal, Gerardo, and Cynthia Y. King. "Neuroimaging Studies Reveal Brain Changes in Posttraumatic Stress Disorder." *Psychiatric Annals* 34, no. 11 (November 2004): pp. 845–856.

Vonnegut, Kurt. *A Man Without a Country* (New York: Seven Stories Press, 2005).

Weil, Andrew. *Eating Well for Optimum Health* (New York: Perennial Currents, 2001).

Winnicott, D.W. *The Maturational Processes and the Facilitating Environment: Studies in the Theory of Emotional Development* (London: Karnac Books, 1990).

Winokur, Jon. *Writers on Writing* (Philadelphia: Running Press, 1990).

Index